M000107707

Evangelism Today and Tomorrow

Evangelism

Today
& Tomorrow

Charles L. Chaney
& Granville Watson

COMPILERS/CONTRIBUTERS

BROADMAN PRESS
NASHVILLE, TENNESSEE

© Copyright 1993 ● Broadman Press
All rights reserved
4211-58
ISBN: 0-8054-1158-5

Dewey Decimal Classification Number: 269.2
Subject Heading: EVANGELISM
Library of Congress Catalog Card Number: 92-14853
Printed in the United States of America

Scripture quotations marked (KJV) are from the *King James Version of the Bible*. Those marked (NASB) are from the *New American Standard Bible*. © The Lockman Foundation, 1960, 1962, 1963, 1968, 1971, 1972, 1973, 1975, 1977. Used by permission. Quotations marked (NIV) are from the Holy Bible, *New International Version*, copyright © 1973, 1978, 1984 by International Bible Society.

Library of Congress Cataloging-in-Publication Data

Evangelism today and tomorrow / compiled by Charles L. Chaney and
Granville Watson.
    p.   cm.
  ISBN 0-8054-1158-5
  1. Evangelistic work. I. Chaney, Charles L., 1934-
II. Watson, Granville, 1936-
BV3795.E923 1993
269'.2—dc20   92-14853
                                                CIP

Foreword

Christianity works. Becoming a Christian is the greatest thing that ever happened to me. The next greatest thing is to see someone else born into the kingdom of God. Since Christianity works in our lives, we need to persuade as many people as we possibly can to become Christians, then apply Christianity—if applied, it will work.

We must be saved ourselves before we can share Christianity with others . . . absolutely sure, with a positive "Yes, I know I am on the road to heaven" knowledge . . . then we can look into the eyes of people we might meet and say, "Let me tell you what happened to me." You cannot tell somebody what happened to you if it has not happened, any more than you can tell a person how to get back from a place where you have never been. It is not complicated, just let it happen. You have to be a Christian before you can do what Christians do.

I was doing a book autograph session the other day, and a local newspaper reporter came to interview me. She wanted me to give her an illustration of how Christianity works. I gave her several, like how I met my wife in a church, and we have been happily married for forty years. This did not seem to satisfy the reporter. She said, "Do you have any other illustrations of how Christianity works?"

About that time I saw my friend Alcus Smith in the line waiting to have a book autographed. I told her about how Alcus had been a car salesman who was an alcoholic, about to lose his job, when I went to his home one night about thirty years ago. I prayed with him, counseled him, and told him I loved him and that God loved him. He was gloriously saved, joined my church, and God helped him whip his drinking problem. He now owns the motor company which was about to fire him.

"Yes," I said, "Christianity really works!"

—Jerry Clower

Preface

Putting this book together has been a labor of joy. I've been blessed by this project of joy because of its purpose. This book is intended to honor Jack Stanton's commitment and ministry. Everyone who knows Jack Stanton calls him, *"Mr. Evangelism."* Jack Stanton's consuming concern is to make Jesus Christ known, to see people come to know Christ, and to follow Him in responsible church membership. His one passion is to introduce people to Christ and then to train believers to introduce others to Christ.

Jack described himself, "What I claim to be is an evangelist, a teller of the good news—that's all I've ever claimed to be." That's not quite right. While he has served Jesus Christ, he has also served his denomination. Jack has pastored churches, served in two state conventions as director of evangelism, and given fifteen years to the evangelism section of the Home Mission Board. Jack Stanton has been, indeed, *"Mr. Evangelism"* for his denomination. For the past fourteen years he has been associated with Southwest Baptist University as the Director of the Institute of Evangelism. During this time, along with his duties in the classroom and in finding resources to help develop an evangelism and conference center at the university, he has continued to be very much the itinerant evangelist. His service as the first vice president of the Southern Baptist Convention for two consecutive years has intensified that itinerant ministry. It has also been a crown on a long life in denominational service. May he serve many more!

A further joy arising from work on this book, for me, has been the privilege of working with those who have contributed to it. The contributors are almost a roll call of honor among modern evangelists. C. E. Autrey is a living legend in evangelism. E. J. Daniels, and Owen Cooper provoked their denomination to creative evangelism efforts. Both were committed to this project before their untimely deaths. Roy Fish, Lewis Drummond, Chuck Kelly, and Leonard Sanderson are superior teachers of evangelism at major seminaries in America. C. B. Hogue and

Larry Lewis are significant leaders of institutions committed to evangelism. Billy Graham has a secure place among American evangelists of the twentieth century. James L. Sells is an outstanding lay teacher and the principal mover in the rise of Southwest Baptist University in the last twenty-five years. His vision of training lay leaders in evangelism brought Jack Stanton to the university. Everyone knows Jerry Clower as an entertainer and motivational speaker with a Christian commitment. Friends know him as a personal witness and soul-winner. He wrote his brief "Foreword" out of appreciation for the tremendous impact that Jack has had in training lay leaders in evangelism.

Finally, I need to say a word about how the book has come together. When we began the process, we wanted to put together a book that would not only honor Jack's ministry but also serve as a brief introduction to evangelism for the college student or the interested layman. I am pleased with what the book has become in that regard. It not only lays the theological foundation for evangelism, but it tends toward the practical and pragmatic, a blend we desperately need today. I believe this book is especially strong in two other areas. The emphasis on the ministry of the laity and the role of personal evangelism in the evangelization of the world is especially prominent. Second, the book has a focus on the vocational evangelist that is especially needed. For years those who wrote about evangelism have almost acted as if the pastor-evangelist was the only kind that existed. All along God has also been calling and using professional evangelists.

Contributors

Some of the material in this book is here by special permission of the authors or publishers.

Roy Fish's chapter is a revision of an article appearing in the Spring 1966 issue of *Southwestern Journal of Theology*, pp. 71-78. C. B. Hogue's chapter is a revision and updating of an article that first appeared in *The Theological Educator*, Spring 1980, pp. 10-18. Owen Cooper was in the midst of writing his chapter when he died. His chapter is taken from the book *Laos: All the People of God*. E. J. Daniel's chapter is revised and condensed material from his *Area Crusade Manual* (revised by Granville Watson).

Billy Graham's chapter is revised slightly and taken from *Decision Magazine.*

Ron Johnson has been so much involved in the production of the chapters by Robert Hamblin and Larry Lewis that he could well be listed as a co-author. I wish to give him a special word of thanks.

Larry L. Lewis was a church planter and pastor in Ohio and Pennsylvania for ten years. He then became director of Religious Education for the Baptist Convention of Pennsylvania-South Jersey. In 1974, he became pastor of the Tower Grove Baptist Church in St. Louis, a declining inner-city church. During his tenure there, the church did a wonderful turn around and became one of the leading churches in evangelism in the Southern Baptist Convention. In 1981, he became president of Hannibal-LaGrange College where he served with distinction until June 1, 1987, when he was named president of the Home Mission Board of the Southern Baptist Convention.

Granville Watson, Jack Stanton's associate in the Jim Mellers Evangelism and Conference Center and the Institute of Evangelism, has not only prepared the chapter on Jack Stanton's life and ministry, he has also revised the chapter by E. J. Daniels for publication.

Carol Nunn, Kathy Johnston, and Melody Whillock, secretaries of the Courts Redford School of Theology at Southwest Baptist University, have entered, altered, added to, and otherwise nurtured these pages through the word-processing procedure with patience and interest. Also, a number of S.B.U. students have helped in the process. A special word of thanks goes to each of them.

Brenda Conway, Administrative Assistant to Dr. Jack Stanton and the International Institute of Evangelism has done the final editing and preparation on the book for publication.

I complete this project with a prayer that God will use this book to bring many to Jesus Christ. *America* must *be Christian!*

Introduction

I was traveling on the interstate toward St. Louis when it happened. In the providence of God it all came together. We would establish a program emphasis in evangelism at Southwest Baptist University, and we would get the best person we could to direct the program. And we did.

The bumper sticker on the car in front of me as I neared the city read, "Honk, if you love Jesus." Now, I had read that sticker many times and always felt a little kinship with the driver ahead of me, but this time anger swelled up in my neck and I said aloud, "That sign ought to say, "Honk if you don't know Jesus." That's evangelism. And that was the nudge I needed.

For many months, I had agonized about the lack of emphasis on evangelism in my convention, in my church, and in the University. Also, I had become deeply convicted about my own failings in personal evangelism.

I had watched my national convention neatly fence in evangelism by tucking it away under some other area of emphasis. I had noted the number of state conventions that had placed evangelism on a lower rung in their structure. I had listened as experienced pastors told me that their seminary education included almost no preparation in practical evangelism, rather was generally a study of the history and role of spiritual awakenings. Our young graduates newly enrolled in some of our seminaries reported that the study of evangelism seemed to have only a minor emphasis. I had grieved as I observed local churches draining the revival from fourteen days to only three days, while other churches replaced revivals with conferences.

I had been confused as I counted the Christian colleges that had abandoned chapel services, had replaced revivals, and had courses in eastern religions but none in evangelism. Had they forgotten that the foundation of Christian higher education was inextricably linked with evangelism? I had cried when I talked to laymen who had no skill and no confidence in sharing their faith. One afternoon, a nationally recognized business leader said to me, "Jim, I couldn't lead one person one step to Jesus

Christ if my life depended on it." And I had grieved when I looked at myself and knew that I had not developed enough personal discipline to adequately equip myself in evangelism. I knew, too, that many of our churches had provided precious few opportunities for training in evangelism along the way.

When I arrived in St. Louis, I called several of our campus leaders to come to the city and join me in prayer and study to develop a sound program in evangelism at SBU and to pray that we would be able to find a nationally recognized leader in evangelism to guide the program. Following prayer and discussion, we were confirmed that we should found an Institute of Evangelism and that Jack Stanton was the best person in America to lead the new effort. Since Jack was already happily employed and almost too busy to find time to talk, we knew it would be difficult. In the providence of God, I met Jack in Virginia the following day and a conversation began that would be continued in a beautiful relationship together in Missouri.

Jack Stanton knew how to preach to the masses and invite them in. He also knew how to write on soul-winning. He had led lay conferences on evangelism across our country. He had held successful revivals on college campuses. He had the biggest heart for evangelism that I had ever known. And he had the warmest and kindest spirit for evangelism that I had ever known.

Course work in evangelism and discipleship became a part of our core requirements at Southwest. Ministerial and other church vocation students took additional course work in evangelism. Revivals and spiritual emphasis programs on our campus were strengthened. Seminars and workshops in evangelism were provided for pastors. Campus revival teams were better equipped. Crusades were put in place. Lay training programs were established. And we developed our overarching goal to train every student to be able to share his faith with skill and clarity. Also, every student would have an opportunity to participate in a cross-cultural mission trip before graduation. We have not been able to do all we ought and all we want to do, but we are on our way. *Jack Stanton has shown us how.*

The Institute of Evangelism was prelude to a strong and comprehensive program we have established in discipleship. A Chair of Church Growth followed. Two new chairs in evangelism are developing. An emphasis in spiritual awakening is emerging, and we believe the Holy Spirit wants to do something afresh in our place. We want to be ready to be used, and Jack Stanton has helped equip us for more useful service.

Many people know Jack Stanton as *"Mr. Evangelism"* while others know him as "Mr. Enthusiasm." Actually he is both. All along the way his wife, Mary, has been both partner and rock. Her influence for good has been felt at Southwest Baptist University, and other people around the world know of her warmth and gentility. This collection of writings adds significantly to the literature of evangelism and honors both Mary and Jack Stanton. I thank the writers for their contributions, Dr. Charles Chaney for his guidance, and the readers for what they will do in evangelism because of the impact of this book.

—James L. Sells

Contents

1 | Jack Stanton: His Ongoing Ministry

Granville Watson

What has energized Dr. Jack Stanton to spend most of his life planning the best ways to reach lost people with the gospel of Jesus Christ? What has motivated him to develop methods of witnessing that allow pastors and laity to become dynamic witnesses of Christ's saving power? This energy and motivation comes from the redemptive power of God.

On August 31, 1919, in East St. Louis, Illinois, Jack Stanton was born into a fatherless home and had to fight for survival. As a young man he came to know Christ when he was a hard-headed, hot-tempered construction worker. For the last forty-one years he has given Southern Baptist Evangelism his gift of leadership. Stanton's compelling need to serve his Lord can be illustrated by the moving description of his salvation experience.

Stanton's Salvation Experience

In his younger years, he became a tough self-reliant young man with little time for God or His church. He dropped out of high school for two years and worked as a truck driver and furnace factory laborer. When telling of his conversion Stanton says, "We didn't go to church except on certain occasions." One day, after re-entering high school, and still working part-time in construction, he went to visit his grandmother in East St. Louis. He went to get a good meal, but also got an invitation to go to revival services at her church. Incensed because she urged him to attend church, his angry response caused her to cry. To make her feel better, he went with her that night. In that revival service, Jack Stanton was first confronted with the gospel of Jesus Christ through personal evangelism. There he also experienced the power of God that would change his life and motivate his ministry. The simple witness of a young man who was a new Christian brought Jack Stanton to Jesus.

> "A young man came to me during the invitation," Jack recalls, "and asked me to receive Christ as my Savior and Lord. I was very upset and yelled at him. In confusion he left me and returned to his seat. A few minutes later he returned to ask me to go down to the front and pray with him. I agreed to go forward when the young man agreed not to take me to the preacher."

Jack asked the young man why he had chosen to talk with him. The young man, known as Brown, related his own personal testimony. He had been saved three nights earlier and had asked God to lead him to witness to someone who needed Christ. "I opened my eyes during the prayer," Brown explained, "and saw you. That is why I am here." He then proceeded to tell Jack how to receive Christ and then how to pray. "Just talk to God like you are talking to me," Brown said. So Jack Stanton bowed his head and prayed, "If you can save me and help me to be a witness where I work, the best I know how, I will give you my life." Jack knew that he had come to a major turning point in his life. As he walked back up the aisle he paused and said, "Thank God, Jack Stanton has been born again."

His Motivation

The motivation and desire to serve God has been evident in Jack Stanton's life from the beginning of his Christian journey. On the night of his conversion he promised God he would witness to everyone he could at school, on the job, and in the community. He recognized the importance of personal evangelism because of the witness of the young man who led him to Jesus.

God called Jack Stanton to preach; he also felt a strong leading of the Holy Spirit to give his life to evangelism. During his college and seminary days he served as pastor of evangelistic churches and preached in many revivals. In 1949 and 1950, he was asked to conduct revivals on the campus of what was then Southwest

Baptist College. God brought about a great spiritual awakening in both of these years. Many students received Jesus Christ as Lord and Savior and scores surrendered to the gospel ministry. The spiritual impact was felt by the entire community. The moving of God in the lives of those students continues to this day and is evidenced by their ministries here in the United States and around the world. These experiences have created a bond between Jack and the ministries that he has undertaken. The anointing of God on his efforts thrusts him into the mainstream of evangelism.

His Mission

The strength for his ministry was discovered after his first speaking attempt. "I remember the first time I spoke, no one responded. I was so broken about it I thought, 'I'll die if I talk about Jesus and there is no response,' so I prayed much," he said. His prayers were answered. The next time he spoke, many people responded by accepting Jesus Christ. Christian friends began to encourage Stanton to become a preacher. "I didn't run from God. I just prayed that God could and would use me," he said. His personal prayer life was enriched by this experience. Encouragement from his wife and his friends solidified the decision to enter the gospel ministry.

After being licensed and ordained by the West Park Baptist Church of St. Louis, Jack Stanton launched his lifelong campaign to spread the gospel. The desire to tell lost people about the saving grace of Jesus Christ is evidenced in every major development of his life. When he married Mary Skrivan of Overland, Missouri, he found a companion, prayer warrior, and encourager for his ministry. Upon completion of high school he attended William Jewell College and then graduated (B.A.) from Shurtleff College in Alton, Illinois. Continuing the quest to prepare himself for the mission of evangelism, he graduated from Central Baptist Theological Seminary (B.D.). At Central he finished his doctoral seminars and later completed his degree at Luther Rice Seminary (Th.D.).

His Methods

With the direction of his life's mission settled, he began to develop Christ-like methods for his evangelism ministry. His goal in ministry has been to imitate the methods of Jesus. Stanton has succeeded in meeting people where they are, sensing their needs, and identifying their problems and defenses, to present the claim of Christ. In 1978, while leading an area-wide evangelistic crusade in Mississippi, he was interviewed on a local television talk show. After the interview was over, he sensed the openness of the talk show host to his testimony. There before the television audience, he shared the message of Christ with that young lady. As they talked, she confessed the hurt and the need in her life. Using Scripture he showed her how Christ could save her and supply the needs of her life. She prayed for Christ to come into her life. His sensitivity to people's needs provides many opportunities for him to share the gospel in this manner. Jesus used this method of witnessing. Stanton practices it in his own life and teaches other Christians to use it also.

His Service

Jack Stanton served as the first Director of Evangelism for the Kansas Convention of Southern Baptists, which included Kansas and eastern Nebraska. There he conducted the first Southern Baptist revival. He also served as the Director of the Colorado Baptist General Convention which included Colorado, Wyoming, Montana, North Dakota, South Dakota, and western Nebraska. His program of lay evangelism revolutionized the involvement of laymen in personal evangelism.

Dr. Jaroy Webber first called Dr. Stanton, "Mr. Evangelism." Dr. Stanton has developed many methods in mass evangelism and in sharing one's personal faith. While he worked at the Home Mission Board in Personal Evangelism, his methodology was developed into programs that have been used around the world.

His Ongoing Ministry

In 1975 Dr. Stanton began serving as the Director of the Institute of Evangelism at Southwest Baptist University in Bolivar, Missouri. This position would provide a way for him to be active in evangelism around the world. By developing a School of Evangelism and a conference center, he ministered, equipped, and encouraged the people of God to be more effective in making Christ known to the world. Jack believes that education and evangelism have walked hand-in-hand since the early years of our country. He points to the Second Great Awakening, about 1800, which began in two little backwoods colleges in Virginia: Hampden-Sydney and Washington. The periods of revival that flowed from the college campuses sparked evangelism across our land. Jack longs to see spiritual awakening happen again with roots deep in the hearts of college students.

Southwest Baptist University is in a unique position to unite evangelism and education in a way that will encourage and equip both individuals and churches in their mission to reach the lost. From its inception SBU has trained its students to reach lost people and equipped them to give Christian leadership wherever they serve. He believes in the SBU staff, faculty, students, friends, pastors, and laity who want to be a vital part of this significant thrust to reach our world with the gospel of Christ. He says, "We have the opportunity. We are in the heart of a tremendous number of small congregations, and at the same time close to some of the fastest growing urban areas of our country."

Jack dreams of another great spiritual awakening in America. He believes spiritual awakening will again begin on our college and university campuses. He desires to become a facilitator in the next great awakening. He says, "We have a climate of recognized need. Almost daily students, laity, and clergy ask for more training in evangelism and for more materials to help them in their efforts."

When putting his ongoing ministry into perspective, one must recall his personal experience, his challenge, his call from God, and his mission. His goal has been to imitate the Master's methods of evangelism. His message has been to present the claims of Christ to people where they are in their lives. He sees the fulfillment of his ongoing ministry through the university campus and the Institute of Evangelism.

Ministry Objectives

Four major objectives form the foundation for the Institute of Evangelism. These objectives have been his guide for formulating the philosophy, plan, and program of the Institute. The ongoing ministry goals are:

1. To develop a conference center and a continuing program of expanded witness training for the laity.
2. To develop classes, seminars, and conferences to train pastors and church vocation personnel in all phases of evangelism with a special emphasis on personal witnessing.
3. To provide training and materials for vocational evangelists.
4. To develop a comprehensive program of evangelism on a college campus and develop an evangelism model for other campuses to follow.

The Jim Mellers Evangelism and Conference Center is physical evidence of Stanton's commitment to establishing a permanent program of evangelism on the SBU campus. The Evangelism and Conference Center was completed in 1984 and dedicated in the spring of 1985 to the ministry of world evangelism. It houses the director and staff offices, the E. J. Daniels Research and Resource Center, the Hyman Appleman Seminar Room, seven classrooms, a library, learning carrels, and the offices of church growth, telecommunication, and university placement. The library facility includes the libraries of Dr. Stanton, Dr. John Havlik and many other pastors, evangelists, and lay persons. The "Hall of Remembrance" was established to preserve the legacy of outstanding evangelists who have given of their leadership abilities and their finances to assist in the development of the Institute of Evangelism.

The Institute of Evangelism is involved in seven areas of ministry:

a. teaching evangelism
b. directing the Jim Mellers Evangelism and Conference Center
c. researching evangelism needs
d. producing evangelistic materials
e. directing an associate evangelistic program
f. developing conferences and crusades
g. forming world evangelism teams to engage in evangelistic activities around the world

Jack sees evangelism as the biblical admonition to put the message of Christ first in the ministry of the church. He says,

Evangelism is the cutting edge of our faith that takes us into the frontiers of an unbelieving world. It is the foundation upon which all of our activities rest. It is the umbrella under which all other activities are gathered. It is the activity that brings people together in the sense of unity, strength, purpose and direction. It will catch the high tide of interest now being shown by Christians everywhere and especially by Southern Baptists as they launch out in the Bold Mission Thrust. It will help us keep in step with the growing awareness of our convention's boards and agencies as they address the needs of the world and prepare for evangelism.

Since coming to Southwest Baptist College in 1975, Stanton has attempted to establish the first academically accredited undergraduate school of evangelism. SBU currently offers a minor in evangelism, with life-style and basic church evangelism as core classes. Courses in church growth and discipleship have enlarged the evangelism study area. Practical training in evangelism is provided through on-campus conferences, seminars, and equipping classes. Eventually a full School of Evangelism will be established.

Training and materials for vocational evangelists has been another emphasis of the initial program of the Institute. The first conference conducted by the Institute was for vocational evangelists and their spouses. Conferences on "Practical Evangelism and Ministry" have been conducted in Memphis, Tennessee, and Oklahoma City, Oklahoma. An annual "Small Congregation Evangelism Conference" was begun in 1984 at the Evangelism and Conference Center. This conference is cosponsored by the Evangelism Division of the Home Mission Board, the Missouri Evangelism Department, the Institute of Evangelism, SBU, and the Henry Roe Evangelism Association of Texas. In addition to these conferences materials related to evangelism and ministry are being developed in the form of printed material and audio/video cassettes.

Another goal is to develop a comprehensive program of evangelism on the SBU campus. The evangelism classes have become cell groups for sharing life-changing experiences, personal needs, and prayer requests. Students have assisted with crusade preparation, evangelism conferences, door-to-door witnessing, and street witnessing as a result of the program sponsored by the Institute of Evangelism. The Institute works closely with the director of University Ministries to assure both academic and spiritual excellence at SBU. Several colleges have sought Jack Stanton's advice about how to develop an Institute of Evangelism or a center for World Evangelism.

His Message

Jack Stanton's love for the Lord Jesus Christ is seen in his every endeavor to encourage pastors and laity in their responsibility as life-style evangelists. He follows in the great tradition of Dr. Owen Cooper who sought to interpret the Great Commission as a motivator for everyone to achieve their maximum potential as witnesses. Jack Stanton has preached, taught, written about, and practiced Christian life-style witness as a natural part of his everyday walk with the Lord. Since he heard the call of God, his first love has been to preach the unsearchable riches of the gospel of Jesus Christ.

This book is written to move the reader to practice life-style evangelism. God will be honored if you do. You will be blessed as you live daily in God's presence.

2 | The New Testament Church in Evangelism
Jack Stanton

The New Testament church was not an afterthought in the mind of God. It did not come into existence because the early Christians faced problems. It came to be by design; the church was in the mind of God from the beginning. The church is central in God's plan for growing great, Christ-like people and in using these people to share the good news of Jesus Christ and His offer of redemption and freedom around the world.

What Is the Church?

The church is many things to many people. to some it is simply the gathering of people who know God. To some it is the mystical, invisible relationship that exists among those who love and attempt to serve God. To others it is a fellowship where they can experience renewal. To still others it is an elite club to which special people belong and from which they benefit. To some it is an almost magical place where feelings can be experienced and blessings received. Others see it as the place where historical and religious dogma can be passed on to each generation.

This study will use the following definition of a church: a church is a group of baptized believers in Jesus Christ who covenant together to carry out the will of Christ in the power of the Holy Spirit.

The Origin of the Church

As a young pastor I heard a preacher say, "Pentecost is the birthday of the Church." The statement caught my attention, and I started to repeat it until I analyzed it more carefully. Pentecost is not the birthday of the Church. Pentecost came after Christ's death, burial, resurrection, and ascension. Jesus began to gather His church before Pentecost and even gave instructions about the procedures that were to take place if the fellowship were broken (Matt. 18:15-18). When Jesus was in Caesarea Philippi, He asked His disciples, "Whom do men say that I the Son of man, am?" (Matt. 16:13, KJV).[1] Numerous answers were given, and then He asked:

> But whom say ye that I am? And Simon Peter answered and said, Thou art the Christ, the Son of the living God. And Jesus answered and said unto him, Blessed art thou, Simon Bar-jona: for flesh and blood hath not revealed it unto thee, but my Father which is in heaven. And I say also unto thee, That thou art Peter, and upon this rock I will build my church; and the gates of hell shall not prevail against it. And I will give unto thee the keys of the kingdom of heaven: and whatsoever thou shalt bind on earth shall be bound in heaven: and whatsoever thou shalt loose on earth shall be loosed in heaven (Matt. 16:15-19, KJV).

Literally, the last statement can be translated "Whatsoever you shall bind on earth shall have been bound in heaven." The Church is to carry out on earth what God has ordained and set forth in heaven.

Some would have us believe that Peter alone had the authority of the keys, but the authority Jesus gave to Peter in Matthew 16:19, He conferred upon all of the church in Matthew 18:18. While Jesus was on earth in human form, He called out and organized His church. The New Testament church is the Jesus movement. The church belongs to Jesus. It is twice His. He founded it, and He "gave himself for it" (Eph. 5:25, KJV). The church does not belong to the pastor, the elected officers, the largest givers, the strong leaders, or special groups within its membership. The church belongs to Jesus. He is its head (Eph. 5:23). He loves it (Eph. 5:25). He continues to work in and through His church (Mark 16:20). He will come again for His church and present it to Himself a glorious church (Eph. 5:27). The Lord's church is alive and well and will be here until Jesus returns to claim it as His own.

Christ has promised to build His church. Many congregations look to their pastor and staff to build their church, but this is a tragic mistake. I was in a church with a young, energetic pastor. The leaders in the church said to me, "We are tired of young preachers. They wear us out with all of their activities, and there is little or no growth. What we need is an older preacher who is more stable and has more experience. Then we will grow." I have been in a church with an older pastor. The leaders said, "We are tired of older pastors who have been around so long that they have lost their vision and enthusiasm. We need a young pastor with some get-up-and-go." A person in a small dying congregation said to me, "If we could get Dr. Billy Graham to be our pastor, he would build us a church." God uses humans instrumentally and all of His children must be available to be used in building a church. However, it is the sovereign, omnipotent God who builds the church. He takes the initiative to build His church and He uses chosen vessels. To Him belongs the glory.

Jesus also reminded us that the gates of hell (powers of darkness, authority of death; translate it any way you choose) shall not prevail or stand against the church (Matt. 16:18). This verse does not picture a small group of frightened, defeated believers huddled together singing, "Hold the fort for I am coming." It describes a mighty, militant group of believers so energized by the Holy Spirit that they become effective soldiers of the cross. Praise God, "greater is he that is in you, than he that is in the world" (1 John 4:4, KJV). The church has been called to penetrate every darkened area of its community and lovingly dispel that darkness with heaven's light. The church should obey God and in His power should bind on earth what has been bound in heaven and loose on earth what has been loosed in Heaven (compare Matt. 16:19).

The Commission of the Church

Before Jesus ascended into heaven, He said, "All power is given unto me in heaven and in earth. Go ye therefore, and teach all nations, baptizing them in the name of the Father, and of the Son, and of the Holy Ghost: Teaching them to observe all things whatsoever I have commanded you: and, lo, I am with you alway, even unto the end of the world. Amen" (Matt 28:18-20, KJV). Jesus began His message to His church by declaring that all power was given Him in heaven and in earth. What a remarkable way to begin. He first establishes that the power available in heaven is now available on earth and that through Him there are sufficient resources to enable the church to carry the gospel to the world. He also promised His presence to the end. For the church to stumble in powerlessness on earth means that it is not plugged in to its power source.

Jesus defined the task of the church as threefold. First, the church is to *make disciples*. It is to lead people to repent of sin and receive Jesus Christ as their Lord and Savior. All are to go into all of the world with all of the gospel, all of the time, in all of the power of God. His precious promise is that He will be with us all of the way.

Second, the church is to *mark disciples;* to baptize them. In baptism a person identifies with Jesus and His church. When a person joins one of the armed forces of the United States, he or she is sworn in and is listed as a member of that unit. Later he or she is given a uniform which identifies the person more fully. The uniform doesn't make the person a member; it identifies the person as a member. Baptism serves the same purpose. It identifies the person as a believer and brings them into the fellowship of the church.

Finally, the church has also been called to *mature disciples* through teaching them to observe Christ's commands. So many church members are lost to useful lives and ministries because they have not been taught. Almost any congregation would double its attendance, greatly increase its ministries, and extend its evangelistic outreach if it would teach, train, and involve the members in spiritual growth. The church has been "called out" to do many things. The church is to worship and to minister, but the greatest task of the church is to make disciples.

Some years ago I visited a bottle factory and watched in amazement as bottles were formed, hardened, stamped, boxed, and sent on their way to useful purposes. It was a very profitable business. Suppose I invested in the company. Then, after buying into the company, I was away from it for an extended time. Later when I returned to the factory, I found that the furnace that melted the glass was hot, but there was no liquid glass coming from it. Although each piece of machinery was working perfectly, no bottles were being propelled along the line. The employees were very active, but no bottles were being made, boxed, or sold. Immediately, I would ask the manager, "Where are the bottles?" If he began to tell me of the warmth of the furnace, the deafening roar of the machinery, and the frenzied activity of the people, I would say, "That is all well and good, but I did not invest in warmth, machinery, and activity. I invested in bottles. If there are no bottles, we are out of business."

If I go to a church and ask about the new converts (new bottles), and the pastor says, "Have you noticed the warmth of our fellowship?" I reply, "Yes, but where are the converts?" If the pastor calls attention to the enormous organizations of his church; again I ask, "Where are the converts?" If he reminds me of the unrelenting exercises of his people as they go to all kinds of meetings and functions; I still must ask the question:"Where are the new believers?" The church must remain forever committed to the Lord Jesus Christ and must obey His command to share the gospel with the world. Such commitment will see new believers born into the family of God. The gospel is still "the power of God unto salvation" (Rom. 1:16, KJV). To do anything less than this is spiritual treason and will eventually put the church out of business.

The Church Empowered

Doing God's work without God's power is presumptuous, foolish, and ineffective. After Christ's death, burial, and resurrection but before his ascension, Jesus helped his disciples understand the Scriptures. He declared to them:

> Thus it is written, and thus it behoved Christ to suffer, and to rise from the dead the third day: And that repentance and remission of sins should be preached in his name among all nations, beginning at Jerusalem. And ye are witnesses of these things. and, behold, I send the promise of my Father upon you: but tarry ye in the city of Jerusalem, until ye be endued with power from on high (Luke 24: 46-49, KJV).

God's work must always be performed in God's power.

> For we wrestle not against flesh and blood, but against principalities, against powers, against the rulers of the darkness of this world, against spiritual wickedness in high places (Eph. 6:12, KJV).

The Holy Spirit is the church's power. Following the Spirit's leadership brings the Spirit's power to the church. God empowers the church by giving it Spirit-led leaders who equip the church to do "the work of the ministry" (Eph. 4:12, KJV).

The Church in Evangelism

The first two chapters of the Book of Acts tell the beginning of the story of the church as it continued in what Jesus began both to do and to teach while He was on the earth. We are tempted to think of the early Jerusalem church as a perfect church, set in perfect surroundings, enjoying perfect fellowship. However, that church, was made up of imperfect people; forgiven and redeemed sinners who sought to know and to do the will of God. It was placed in an evil environment which either ignored the church's message or took advantage of every opportunity to destroy it. How did the earliest church survive and grow?

It Overcame Obstacles

The early churches lived in perilous times of great crises and conflicts. The beginning church was small in number, despised by the majority of the population, and without a building in which to meet. At first they were without a pastor. The first treasurer, Judas, turned out to be a traitor and a thief. Peter, a leader of this group, denied he knew Jesus. All of this took place in Jerusalem where Jesus was crucified. The obstacle for effective evangelism was Pentecost itself. During Pentecost the resident families would be inundated by guests and relatives. How could the people worship and witness while caring for their guests? In spite of the many problems and obstacles experienced by the small congregation, the people obeyed God, and God poured out His presence and His power upon His people. If we obey God, we can experience revival and grow an evangelistic church on the very threshold of hell.

It Agonized in Prayer

Someone has said that prayer is the golden chain which links heaven and earth together. We can always do more after we have prayed. A call to evangelize is a call to prayer. Before the evangelistic victory on Pentecost, there were ten agonizing days of confession, intercession, and petition. "These all continued with one accord in prayer and supplication, with the women, and Mary the mother of Jesus, and with His brethren" (Acts 1:14, KJV). We must call our people to prayer. Through confession and repentance we can become clean, open channels and God's presence and power can mobilize us to help others.

It Studied the Scriptures

Confused, and yet challenged, by all they had been through, the people of the earliest churches sought a sure word from God that would help them interpret the activities of the past and plan for the future. They found explanations and help in the Word of God. God has given us the Bible to help us understand the uncertainties around us and to help us chart a safe course to victory.

The Bible is still more modern and up-to-date than tomorrow's newspaper. In its pages, God speaks to us concerning the great issues of life and offers us abundant, eternal life through His Son.

> And in those days Peter stood up in the midst of the disciples, and said, (the number of names together were about an hundred and twenty). Men and brethren, this Scripture must needs have been fulfilled, which the Holy Ghost by the mouth of David spake before concerning Judas, which was guide to them that took Jesus (Acts 1:15-16, KJV).

Peter answered the charges that the strange actions and activities that occurred on the day of Pentecost were the result of drunkenness produced by new wine. He turned to the Word of God and declared, "this is that which was spoken by the prophet Joel" (Acts 2:16, KJV). Then he explained from the Scriptures the good news of the redemptive acts of God in Christ Jesus and offered them the salvation available through Christ. To be effective evangelists, we must love, know, live, and share the Word of God.

It Organized for Evangelism

Acts 1:16-26 describes how the church came together in a business meeting to discuss some of their problems and to elect someone to take the place of Judas. They felt they must organize more fully to meet the opportunities of service and witness that were before them. They did not feel that organization is nonspiritual. They believed God was a God of order. The early church followed God's example to do its work and worship in an orderly manner.

Lack of organization is far more an evidence of carelessness and even laziness than it is of spirituality. The church must discipline itself to take what God has provided and, under His leadership, organize it so that the church can be more effective in reaching the world for Christ. Proper organization helps us serve the Lord.

It United for Strength

The church came together and united in a common goal (Acts 2:1). The church must come together because of inner compassion and not be driven together by outer compulsion. Our common concerns to love Christ, to obey Him, and to share Him with others must unite us. Our common goal must be to win our world to Christ. We can always do more together than we can separately.

It Depended on the Spirit

Our best efforts apart from the presence and power of the Holy Spirit are faulty and fruitless. Before Jesus departed from this earth, He said He would send the Holy Spirit who would "reprove the world of sin, and of righteousness, and of judgment" (John 16:8, KJV). The Holy Spirit helps the lost person understand that not believing Jesus is the great damning sin. He helps the lost person get a view of righteousness, or how to live right, and of judgment because the evil one is already judged. Only the Holy Spirit can make these great truths understandable to a lost person.

Jesus said, "Except a man be born of water and of the Spirit, he cannot enter into the kingdom of God" (John 3:5, KJV). The Holy Spirit effects the new birth in lost persons and brings them into the family of God. Jesus revealed that "when he, the Spirit of truth, is come, he will guide you into all truth" (John 16:13, KJV). The Holy Spirit lives within the believer to offer help for the crises that occur in the daily activities of life.

The New Testament church took seriously the commission Jesus gave them. The church felt a responsibility of sharing the gospel with the whole world. They remembered that Jesus said, "But ye shall receive power, after that the Holy Ghost is come upon you: and ye shall be witnesses unto me both in Jerusalem, and in all Judea, and in Samaria, and unto the uttermost part of the earth" (Acts 1:8, KJV). As the church obeyed God, "they were all filled with Holy Ghost, and began to speak with other tongues, as the Spirit gave them utterance" (Acts 2:4, KJV). As members of His church today, we too have been commanded to be filled with the Holy Spirit (Eph. 5:18).

It Publicized the Event

Acts 2:6 is an interesting verse. It reads, "Now when this was noised abroad, the multitude came together" (KJV). What brought the multitude together? There are various interpretations of this verse, but whatever the cause, the result was that a multitude gathered, and heard the gospel preached. About 3,000 people were saved and baptized. (Compare Rom. 10:14,17.)

The church of today needs to re-think its media approach to the lost. Much of our publicity is self–serving and presents no appeal or challenge to those without Christ. Because of the desperate condition of those apart from Christ, the church needs to take advantage of every opportunity to publicize the good news in a way that honors God and blesses and helps the lost.

It Evangelized

The fire of God fell upon the gathered people on the day of Pentecost (Acts 2:3). God's fire burned brightly, not only above the believers, but also deep within them. Courageously they bore witness to the wonderful works of God, and Peter declared that the Jesus whom they had crucified was both Lord and Christ. Convicted by the bold proclamation of the gospel, the multitudes cried out:

> What shall we do? Then Peter said unto them, Repent, and be baptized every one of you in the name of Jesus Christ for the remission of sins, and ye shall receive the gift of the Holy Ghost. For the promise is unto you, and to your children, and to all that are afar off, even as many as the Lord our God shall call. And with many other words did he testify and exhort, saying, Save yourselves from this untoward generation. Then they that gladly received his word were baptized: and the same day there were added unto them about three thousand souls (Acts 2:37-41, KJV).

Praise God for the gospel. When it is preached in its fullness and in the power of the Holy Spirit, remarkable things happen and lives are changed forever. This great ingathering took place not only because of the fearless public proclamation of the gospel by Peter but also because of the winsome and effective personal witness of the 120 disciples.

When the apostle Paul preached on Mar's Hill, only a few responded to the gospel (Acts 17:22,34). Does this mean Peter was the great, fiery evangelist and Paul was the quiet, intelligent theologian? That Peter brought men to faith in Christ and Paul built them up in the faith? Absolutely not. Paul was one of the greatest evangelists of all times, and Peter was a great theologian. Paul bore his witness for Christ all alone and in the midst of a hostile environment. In spite of the difficulties, some people believed and were saved (v. 34). Thank God for the brave people at home and abroad, who go alone into strange environments and lovingly share Christ. The results may not be spectacular numerically, but they are everlasting spiritually.

Peter had the advantage in that he had a large, responsive crowd gathered and 120 personal witnesses active in sharing Christ. One of the outstanding mass evangelists of our day says about 85 percent of the people who come forward in mass meetings at night have already been led to Christ through personal witnessing before the crusade begins.

It Congregationalized

A burning ember plucked from its flaming bed of coals and isolated will soon cool and die. The early church members knew they needed each other, so they "continued steadfastly" (Acts 2:42, KJV) together. The New Testament church sought to know and to do the Word of God. They continually listened to the teaching of the apostles.

The church enjoyed great fellowship. The members were held together by a common interest and sought diligently to help one another. Fellowship involves total commitment to each other and active participation in a common goal. The early church remembered Christ's sacrificial death and His admonition, "For as often as ye eat this bread, and drink this cup, ye do shew the Lord's death till he come" (1 Cor. 11:26, KJV). They celebrated the Lord's Supper by breaking bread and drinking the cup.

To the early believers, prayer was their communication system; they spoke to God and God spoke to them. They met together for worship and witness. They gained confidence and strength from each other. Power is generated when Christ meets with His gathered people to revive, reaffirm, and reassign them.

Joy was a trademark of the early Christians. The gladness reflected in each life radiated throughout the congregation when they assembled. Their contagious happiness stood in stark contrast to the gloomy conditions surrounding them. Our joy must be drawn from Christ rather than from our present surroundings. Praise was always on the lips of the New Testament believers.

The people praised God in their assemblies and as they went about their daily activities.

The early church met in a spirit of awe and reverence. The church bowed down and humbled itself before God. In some churches today, God is commanded to perform as if the church were in charge of the universe. Christ has given us great gifts and privileges. We must remember we serve a holy and righteous God, and we are His servants.

Exciting things continued to happen as the church came together—"many wonders and signs were done by apostles" (Acts 2:43b, KJV). God is the same yesterday, today, and forever. He is still working miracles in the midst of His believing people. The church continued to grow spiritually and numerically. Its members witnessed for Christ by the words they spoke, by the lives they lived, and by the love they manifested. The fantastic growth of the New Testament church came because the members loved God with all of their heart, believed God with all of their mind, served God with all of their strength, obeyed Him with all of their will, and did all of this through the presence and power of the Holy Spirit.

Common concern for each other led the early Christians to make enormous sacrifices in order that all might benefit. Some were not willing to have so much while others had so little.

As glorious as the past has been, the church of today faces even greater challenges and blessings. The church must continue to share the gospel around the world until the kingdoms of this world become the kingdoms of our God.

3 | The Gift and Calling of the Evangelist

Billy Graham

Some evangelists serve in places that are unreceptive to the gospel. They get discouraged because there seems to be so few results and wonder if it is worthwhile to continue preaching. Some evangelists have family problems and some face overwhelming temptations and trials. On the other hand, some have seen hundreds, even thousands, come to Christ through the preaching of the gospel. Regardless of the number of responses to the gospel, they are all evangelists whom God has called to the ministry of evangelism.

If God has given you the gift of an evangelist and has called you to proclaim the gospel, you must be faithful to that gift and that calling God Himself has given you. The evangelistic harvest is always urgent. We must prepare the ground, sow the seed of God's Word and water it. The apostle Paul declared to the Corinthians, "I have planted, Apollos watered; but God gave the increase" (1 Cor. 3:6, KJV).

We are facing a period of unprecedented harvest for the gospel. Many people are disillusioned because secular answers have failed them. They have tried everything in their desperate search for peace and security—materialism, politics, drugs, alcohol, sex, money, the occult, Satan worship, false philosophies and religions—and they have all failed. Millions of people are open to the message of hope and new life in Christ. We could see the greatest harvest for the gospel our world has ever seen.

This harvest time is also due to world events. Almost every newspaper and book indicate "The harvest is ripe" (see John 4:35). Jesus spoke of a time when there would be "upon the earth distress of nations, with perplexity; the sea and the waves roaring; Men's hearts failing them for fear, and for looking after those things which are coming on the earth" (Luke 21:25-26, KJV). He could well have been describing our generation. Seldom has the soil of the human heart and mind been better prepared. The words of Jesus challenge Christians as never before: "behold, I say unto you, Lift up your eyes, and look on the fields; for they are white already to harvest" (John 4:35, KJV). Harvest time lasts only a short time. If there is no harvest, then ripeness turns to rottenness and the crop is lost. We read in Proverbs 10:5, "He that gathereth in summer is a wise son: but he that sleepeth in harvest is a son that causeth shame."

The Gift and the Call of the Evangelist

The gift of evangelism is often neglected—it is not taught in many Bible schools and seminaries. There are many definitions for evangelism and for what an evangelist is. Some think of evangelism as simply getting more people to join the church. Others define evangelism as attempting to change the structures of society. There are those who have moved from a belief in people's personal, moral responsibility before God to a concept which declares that all people are saved. They say humans are not lost, there is no Judgment Day, there is no hell. Unless we believe in a future judgment and that people are lost without Christ, then the cutting edge of evangelism is blunted.

That brings us to the crucial question of defining an evangelist. An evangelist is a person with a special gift and a special calling from the Holy Spirit to announce the good news of the gospel. It is a gift of God. "He gave some, apostles; and some, prophets; and some, evangelists; and some, pastors and teachers" (Eph. 4:11, KJV). It cannot be manufactured, organized, or manipulated. It is a calling from God. Understanding this will save us from two dangerous temptations. First, it will save us from pride. The gifts we have and the opportunities open to us are from God. We cannot take any credit or glory for ourselves. Secondly, it will save us from discouragement, because we know our calling is from God. As Paul said, "For though I preach the gospel, I have nothing to glory of: for necessity is laid upon me; yea, woe is unto me, if I preach not the gospel!" (1 Cor. 9:16, KJV).

The gift of the evangelist, as outlined in Ephesians 4, is just as important as being a teacher or a pastor, and is just as valid a gift today as it was in the early decades of the Christian church. The church needs to recognize and recover the legitimacy and importance of the gift and the calling of the evangelist.

The term *evangelism* encompasses every effort to declare the good news of Jesus Christ, to the end that people may understand God's offer of salvation and respond in repentance, faith, and discipleship. But we must always make it clear that there is a "cost" to following Christ. There is the denial of self and the taking up of a cross. Christ never offers cheap grace. He never lowers His standard for entrance into the kingdom of God.

The Motives of the Evangelist

One motive of an evangelist is love. Paul, the apostle was proof. He said, "The love of Christ constraineth us" (2 Cor. 5:14, KJV). The greatest act of love we can ever perform for other persons is to tell them about God's love for them in Christ. Missionaries throughout the world carry the message of Christ's redeeming love. Hospitals, schools, orphanages, and leprosariums have been built followed by hundreds of other good works. Many missiologists will admit the mistakes some missionaries have made in various parts of the world, but it is quite easy to criticize them in hindsight! Hundreds of them were separated from loved ones for years on end. Hundreds suffered martyrdom in order to bring the light of the gospel to various parts of the world. Early missionaries brought the message of the gospel to the United States, and I thank God for them.

The approaching Judgment is another motive for our evangelism. Paul said, "Knowing therefore the terror of the Lord, we persuade men" (2 Cor. 5:11, KJV). When Paul preached his great sermon on Mars' Hill in Athens, he said, "God ... commandeth all men every where to repent: Because he hath appointed a day, in the which he will judge the world in righteousness by that man whom he hath ordained" (Acts 17:30-31, KJV). There is a Judgment Day approaching. The Judge will be Jesus.

In recent years many have rejected the Bible doctrine claiming people are individually sinners before God and will be held responsible to Him at the Judgment. Instead, they believe in a doctrine of collective sinfulness and of the corporate guilt of society. I accept the fact that sin affects society as a whole, and we must take that seriously. However, we are in danger of neglecting the need for personal repentance of sin and of faith in the Lord Jesus Christ. Our primary motive, in my view, is the command of our Commander-in-Chief, the Lord Jesus Christ. We engage in evangelism today, not because we want to, or because we choose to, or because we like to, but because we have been commanded to. We are under orders. Evangelistic inactivity is disobedience. When Paul stood on trial before King Agrippa, Paul recounted God's call to him on the Damascus road. He told the king, "I was not disobedient unto the heavenly vision" (Acts 26:19, KJV). May we have the same kind of obedience that Paul had.

The Message of the Evangelist

A few years ago I listened to one of the greatest challenges to me that I have ever had. We were just beginning our Crusade in Osaka, Japan. At a wonderful reception for us with hundreds of leaders of Osaka and Kyoto, the Governor of Osaka Prefecture turned to me and asked, "Dr. Graham, 2,000 years ago Jesus Christ was born. Why is only one percent of Japan Christian? I think it is because Christians have not made their message clear to the Japanese people."

I challenge you to make the message clear. There are millions for whom the gospel has not been made clear. We have failed in our communication, and people have only a hazy idea of what it means to be a true follower of Jesus Christ.

Several months ago a friend of mine sat in a hut in a Masai village in East Africa, talking with an evangelist who had just completed a walking trip of 110 miles among the remote villages of his people. My friend asked the evangelist, "How do you explain to the Masai how much God loves them?"

The evangelist replied, "My people love their animals, especially their cattle, very much. If one of their cows becomes lost, they will not rest until it is found and brought back safely with the others. I will tell them the story that Jesus told about the shepherd who had 99 sheep safe in the fold and went out to look for the one that was lost. Then they understand how much God loves them and what Jesus did for them when He died on the cross."

That evangelist knew how to make the message clear. He had

correctly "contextualized" the message so that the Masai could understand.

Jesus Christ used simple, everyday stories to make the gospel clear and plain. The apostle Paul summarized our message: "Moreover, brethren, I declare unto you the gospel which I preached unto you, which also [we] have received, . . . that Christ died for our sins according to the scriptures; And that he was buried, and that he rose again the third day according to the scriptures" (1 Cor. 15:1-4, KJV).

Biblical evangelism is committed to the full and final authority of Scripture alone. Our authority is not based upon our experiences, or upon our traditions, or upon the latest ideas of philosophers or politicians. Our authority and our message are solely based on what God has revealed to us in the Bible. In boldness we can proclaim, "Thus saith the Lord." Biblical evangelism preaches Christ alone is the Savior of people. Paul told the Corinthians, "For I determined not to know any thing among you, save Jesus Christ, and him crucified" (1 Cor. 2:2, KJV). The message includes that Jesus alone is the way to God and apart from Him we are spiritually dead and lost. By His death and resurrection, Jesus Christ became the gospel.

The gospel is not just a new set of morals or a guide for happy living. It is the solemn message that by sin we are alienated from God, and only Christ by His death and resurrection can save us. Any message other than the gospel of Jesus Christ is not evangelism. If you preach any other message, you are not an evangelist.

We should go to our various places of service singing a new song as recorded in Revelation: "And they sung a new song, saying, Thou are worthy . . . for thou wast slain, and hast redeemed us to God by thy blood out of every kindred, and tongue, and people, and nation; And hast made us unto our God kings and priests: and we shall reign on the earth" (Rev. 5:9-10, KJV).

We say with John, "Worthy is the Lamb that was slain to receive power, and riches, and wisdom, and strength, and honour and glory, and blessing" (Rev. 5:12, KJV).

That is our message *Worthy is the Lamb.*

4 | Missing Thrust in Today's Evangelism: A Southern Baptist Case Study
Roy Fish

Through the years, Southern Baptist churches have been a mighty force in evangelism. This is proven by the number of people won to Christ and baptized into the fellowship of churches affiliated with the Southern Baptist Convention: 3,900,000 between 1956-1965; 3,950,000 between 1966-1975; and 3,800,000 between 1976-1985. Even though evangelical efforts have been successful, some questions should be asked periodically. First, what might be done presently to increase effectiveness in evangelism? What changes would be most advantageous in an effort to obey the commission of the risen Christ? Are there certain thrusts in any effective program of evangelism which need more emphasis? Do major adjustments in the basic concepts need to be made? Should there be a return to the basics in New Testament evangelism?

Our Basic Evangelistic Thrusts

For a majority of Southern Baptist history, the two basic thrusts in evangelism have been educational evangelism and revival evangelism. Educational evangelism is an effort to get the good news of Jesus to people by enrolling them in a component of a church program, usually the Sunday School. Revival evangelism is the method of using a set period of time for special services of evangelistic emphasis. The importance and effectiveness of these two elements should not be overlooked.

Regarding educational evangelism, John Sisemore says, "As much as 85 percent of all the professions of faith in most Southern Baptist churches come directly through the Sunday School."[1] Undoubtedly, educational evangelism is the most effective method of evangelism employed in the twentieth century. This fact is substantiated by the relationship between the number of people enrolled in Sunday Schools and the number of people who make public decisions for Christ. Failure to enroll people in Sunday Schools noticeably reduces the number of people reached for Christ. For instance, during a fifteen year period in Texas, with the exception of two years, the number of baptisms increased or decreased in direct proportion to the net enrollment in Sunday School. This has often been the case across the entire Southern Baptist Convention.

Revival evangelism still constitutes a very effective method in the Southern Baptist program of evangelism. Churches which employ proper spiritual and practical preparation for a series of special evangelistic services, still find revival evangelism a successful thrust in reaching lost people.

The Limitations of the Basic Thrusts

The limitations of these basic thrusts, educational evangelism and revival evangelism, must be investigated. The basic limitations of these two approaches are: first, only a small percentage of people in an average church field will hear the Christian message; second, churches have shifted the responsibility of delivering the Great Commission.

Suppose a church has one thousand lost people in its church field. These constitute the evangelistic prospects of that church. The Great Commission is to give every one of the thousand prospects an opportunity to hear the gospel. The church is responsible for seeing that each one learn how the abundant and eternal life Christ offers may be received. Can these two methods achieve the goal of evangelizing all the prospects?

The average church would enlist from 10 to 20 percent of its prospects by employing educational evangelism. For a hypothetical church, 15 percent would equal 150 people enrolled in Sunday School. Of this number, most churches would reach one of every three for Christ. Through educational evangelism the church would evangelize 150 of its one thousand prospects and would reach 50 of them for salvation. This leaves a huge majority of the prospects unevangelized.

Revival evangelism will not reach most prospects not already enlisted in the Sunday School. In recent years the lament often heard is, "We just can't get the lost people to our services any more." Our evangelistic thrust is limited due to the kind of religion it represents: a "come and hear" religion. People often say, "Come and hear the gospel taught in our church" or "Come and hear our evangelist preach the gospel." This "come and hear" kind of religion constitutes a reversal of the Great Commission of Jesus. His instructions to His church were not to invite people to "come and hear" but for believers to "go and tell." The main responsibility is not to bring the lost to the gospel but to take the gospel to the lost. Jesus wants us to go and witness, but we have interpreted it to mean, "Go and invite people to church."

The Missing Thrust

There is a missing thrust in evangelism. The missing thrust is one of personal evangelism by well-trained lay witnesses. This void is proven by the fact that it takes 29 Southern Baptists a year to win one person to an open commitment to Christ. A generous estimate would be that approximately five percent of Southern Baptists are effectively sharing the good news of Jesus Christ with others. This is far short of the Lord's intention. Christ intended for every believer to communicate the faith to others.

The church has been powerful during the periods in which the laymen of the church have responded to the commission of Jesus to witness. The first three centuries are regarded as the period during which the church was at its best. Dr. Kenneth Scott Latourette writes: "The chief agents in the expansion of Christianity appear not to have been those who made it a profession or a major part of their occupation, but men and women who earned their livelihood in some purely secular manner and spoke of their faith to those whom they met in this natural fashion."[2]

During the third and fourth centuries, the concept of evangelization gradually changed. The change was due to an enlarged emphasis upon the distinction between the "clergy" and the "laity." Gradually, the task of witnessing was completely taken from the laity and placed into the hands of the clergy. Thus, the plan of Christ was distorted, to a large extent, for an entire millennium. The power of personal evangelism was lost for more than 10 centuries. In spite of enthusiastic slogans and passionate appeals, the concept of a witnessing laity has rarely gripped Christendom with any force during the last 1700 years. Even in a year of emphasis on proclamation and witness, there are very few churches that have even a dozen trained witnesses who can effectively present Christ to others. This missing thrust of committed people is a critical need for the revival of personal evangelism.

Reasons for the Missing Thrust

The great and almost unlimited lay potential has not been tapped for the purpose of evangelism. These laypeople have not been properly trained for witnessing. At present, only a small number of churches are employing any systematic method of training believers for the work of personal evangelism. The evangelistic training given by most churches is of such a general and "scattershot" nature that the percentage of effective lay witnesses trained is smaller every year. A strong emphasis on training lay witnesses would represent a reversal of emphasis in most churches. However, this revolutionary emphasis is a necessity.

Neglecting this kind of training constitutes careless disobedience to a vital part of our Lord's commission. The inevitable fruits are a declining number of converts and spiritually weak churches. Southern Baptists have been busily engaged in making professed disciples and leading them to the baptismal waters. This is a vital part of the Great Commission. However, there has been an embarrassing neglect of the part of the commission which reads "teaching them to observe all things whatsoever I have commanded you." Jesus commanded His disciples to make disciples. In turn, He then instructed them to teach those who had become disciples to obey His commands. Their obedience would lead them to make other disciples. Jesus also commands believers today to make disciples who will in turn witness to others.

Southern Baptists have blundered in considering evangelism as essential and the training of new Christians to be witnesses as optional. This neglect is a major factor in our present dilemma. If converts desire training to a limited degree, they can obtain it. If they do not have spiritual vision enough to see the need of training, or if they do not have spiritual hunger enough to desire it, we simply let them drift into spiritual uselessness. Witnessing and training are immovable parts of the plan our Lord has for reaching the world with the gospel. Training Christians to be witnesses no longer can be an optional matter. The witness itself is seriously impaired when the newly won disciple is not trained to witness effectively to others.

Supplying the Missing Thrust

The key to a successful program of training is the pastor. According to Ephesians 4:11-12, training Christians is the primary purpose of a pastor's ministry. "And these were his gifts: ... some pastors and teachers, to equip God's people for work in his service, to the building up of the body of Christ" (NEB). This passage proves the responsibility for Christian service belongs to the members of the body while the pastor's responsibility is to equip the body for service. The best method for building up the church is witnessing for Christ. Regarding this vital aspect of a pastor's ministry, J. E. Conant has said: "The conclusion is inevitable. The main business of the pastor is not the preparation and delivery of sermons and addresses so much as the development, whether by sermon or by any other method, of every member in his church into a soul-winner. His sermons—at least those to Christians—ought always to have this in view."[3]

Establishing an adequate program for training effective witnesses will be new for most pastors and churches. The successfulness of the programs will be only gradual. The initial effort of training people may be numerically small and consequently inglorious. Remember, Jesus spent most of His earthly ministry training twelve men. After they were adequately trained, the world felt the impact of their ministry. A pastor should select a very few at first and train them well. They must be trained so thoroughly that they can lead and train others. When this is done, a perpetual training program will be effected and an increasing number of adequately trained witnesses will be produced.

During an interview with a representative of the magazine *Christianity Today*, Billy Graham recognized the possibilities of a perpetual training program when employed properly in a church. He was asked the question, "If you were a pastor of a large church in a principal city, what would be your plan of action?" Mr. Graham answered:

I think one of the first things I would do would be to get a small group of eight or ten or twelve men around me that would meet a few hours a week and pay the price! It would cost them something in time and effort. I would share with them everything I have, over a period of a couple of years. Then I would actually have twelve ministers among the laymen who in turn could take eight or ten or twelve more and teach them. I know one or two churches that are doing that, and it is revolutionizing the church. Christ, I think, set the pattern. He spent most of his time with twelve men. He didn't spend it with great crowds. In fact, it seems to me that every time He had a great crowd there were not too many results. The great results, it seems to me, came in His personal interviews and in the time He spent with His twelve.[4]

Until there is a willingness to incorporate a thorough training program in the churches, the overall effectiveness of any denomination will likely continue to decline. Is it too late to realize that effective Christians cannot be produced by assembly-line methods? Long hours of private instruction are essential.

In a day of numerical and spiritual decline, it is heartening to hear some leaders boldly predict that we are standing on the threshold of the greatest era. If we move according to God's plan now, there is a guarantee of greatness and effectiveness in the future. An integral part of His plan is "teaching them to observe all things whatsoever I have commanded."

Notes

1. John T. Sisemore, *The Ministry of Visitation* (Nashville: Broadman Press, 1954), 86.

2. Kenneth Scott Latourette, *A History of the Expansion of Christianity,* Vol. I in *The First Five Centuries* (New York: Harper & Brothers, 1937), 116.

3. J. E. Conant, *Every Member Evangelism for Today* (New York: Harper & Brothers, 1922), 17.

4. Billy Graham, "Billy Graham Speaks: The Evangelical World Prospect," *Christianity Today* III: 1 (October 13, 1958): 5.

5 | A Theology of Evangelism
C. E. Autrey

Some Christians do not know or care much about theology. They fear that it is an enemy. This concept of theology comes from the idea of a cold, stilted, or combative manner in Christian doctrine. This concept is a disservice to most theologians.

The theologian knows that if it were not for evangelism, the outreach of the church, there would be no students for seminary classes. Most evangelists realize that to preach the gospel we must know what it is. The "evangel" is the message. Theology defines our evangel. If we have a well-defined evangel, we will preach it with understanding and clarity. Those listening to the message will grasp it and yield more readily to it. A blurred message produces a blurred response.

All who are converted should know what happened to them and why. They will not know and will be ineffective Christians if we fail to teach them. This again is where theology clarifies the conceptual situation and makes for effective Christian teaching and living. Theology is to evangelism what the steel framework of a huge building is to the edifice.

A knowledge of the theological ramifications of the Christian religion will enable the evangelist to be effective. However, this knowledge without divine compulsion will have very little practical value and will not be used of God.

A person with a burning passion for the lost and no knowledge of the great redemptive facts may successfully use certain evangelistic methods which are incongruous with the gospel. This may result in irreparable damage. It is essential to teach our people a theology of evangelism and give God a chance to create the divine urge. There is no sense in risking a shabby approach when we have access to the balanced truth and the constraining love of God.

Christian Theology

The word *theology* is derived from two Greek words: *theos* for God and *logos* for word. Theology is a word about God. It is a study of God. Christian theology includes more than a study of God; it includes God's relation to humans and the universe. Dr. E. Y. Mullins said theology "has come to mean the whole range of doctrines regarding God in his relations to man."[1]

The *theology* of evangelism is a study of God's relations to all people in the universe. God's relation to His people is peculiarly different from His relation to other people. His people are part of His family while others are not. All people could be members of God's family, if properly related to Him. God is "not willing that any should perish, but that all should come to repentance" (2 Pet. 3:9, KJV). His plan is to become the God to all people through His people (Gen. 12:3; Matt. 28:19-20). In the New Testament His method to become the God of all is evangelism and missions (Acts 1:8; Luke 24:47-49). The *evangel* is the gospel. Jesus Christ is the subject of the gospel, and the Holy Spirit is the power, but God's people are the instruments.

We follow our concept of theology as we speak of "a theology of evangelism." We are speaking in this chapter of truths about God and His relation to the individuals and churches in the field of outreach. We study the origin, development, and teachings of evangelism as it relates to God and His people.

Origin of Evangelism

Jews in the Old Testament knew a partial evangelism. God often visited them with revival. An Old Testament revival was a spiritual upsurge characterized by deep conviction and a strong turning to God. The revival of the Hebrews who were enslaved in Egypt gave the people, with a slave mentality, a force of character they did not have before. The spiritual turning to God gave them the determination to attempt an impossible feat. In every revival of the Old Testament, God's people were enabled to arise from disaster to heights of spiritual revival and prosperity. The revival during Hezekiah's day is an excellent example (2 Chron. 29:1-36; 30:1-27; 32:1-21).

Evangelism comes from God. Pentecost was a new and strong departure in evangelistic outreach. On the day of Pentecost Peter preached to that large audience made up of people from many nations. He did it because God led him. Peter did not plan it. The people came to celebrate the annual feast of Pentecost. God arranged for Jesus' disciples to see Him in His resurrection body for 40 days and to behold Him as He ascended from the slopes of the Mount of Olives to heaven. He let them pray ten days in the upper room. Then He poured out His Spirit upon the disciples as the prophet Joel had said. Peter, moved by the Holy Spirit, preached Jesus, and the power of God moved among them. It was all the plan of God, and about 3,000 people were converted. This happening at Pentecost in its totality is evangelizing. All of the elements of evangelizing are brought out in this experience.

1. The Holy Spirit was poured out upon the disciples. Peter stood up under the power of the Spirit and preached Jesus.

2. Peter proclaimed Jesus Christ as Savior and Lord. Peter said:

a) that Jesus of Nazareth is a man "approved of God" (Acts 2:22) and that He is the "Holy One" (v. 27).

b) that "God hath made this same Jesus, whom ye have crucified, both Lord and Christ" (v. 36).

c) that the Jews had crucified Him (Acts 2:23; Matt. 26:24; Luke 22:22), according to God's foreknowledge and plan.

d) that God raised Him from the dead (Acts 2:24).

3. Peter urged them to come to Christ for salvation (Acts 2:38). "Then they that gladly received his word were baptized: and the same day there were added unto them about three thousand souls" (Acts 2:41, KJV). Peter was standing for Christ, and he pled with them to present themselves to Jesus.

The definition of evangelism consists of these three elements. If you leave out any one of the statements, you do not have evangelism. There is no evangelism without the presence and power of the Holy Spirit. There is no evangelism apart from the proclamation of Jesus Christ as Savior and Lord. There will never be evangelism unless sinners are exhorted to turn to Jesus Christ from sin.

Evangelism, whether it is in the form of revival or witnessing, comes from God. He employs many occasions and different personalities. One can see from a study of the revivals of the Old Testament, compared to the evangelism in the New Testament, that a magnificent advancement took place on the day of Pentecost.

Essential Doctrines of Evangelism

Human Sinfulness

As God's people evangelized in both the Old and New Testaments, they confronted a vicious obstacle: sin in its many forms. We cannot here give a full theological dissertation on sin, but we must look at the nature, the results, and the remedy for sin. Sin is the devil's instrument to drive a wedge between God and people. Sin is a transgression of the law (Rom. 5:12). Sin is unbelief (Rom. 14:23). Sin is willful rebellion against God (Isa. 63:10). Sin is lying to God (Acts 5:1-10). Sin is a bondage. Sin is an awful allurement. Sin is a fundamental wrongness within; it is selfishness and greed. Sin is more than satanic; it is a personal demonic force which enslaves people. Sin will destroy any person, or any civilization, when it is uncurbed and left to run rampant.

A person is a sinner by nature, by choice, and by practice. A sinner cannot charge all personal sins to inherent weakness, for the sinner willfully chooses to sin and is held accountable.

A person is a sinner by nature. To Jeremiah, the unregenerated individual had a nature adverse to God (Jer. 17:9). To Jesus, the unsaved individual was lost (Luke 19:10). Christ went further when He said, "Ye are of your father the devil, and the lusts of your father ye will do" (John 8:44, KJV). Jesus did not regard a person who had not had a transforming experience with God as being part of the family of God. A person has an adverse nature and so stands outside of the family of God. Paul said that believers before the transformation in Christ "were by nature the children of wrath even as others" (Eph 2:3, KJV).

A person is also a sinner by choice. Each individual willfully chooses sin and is held accountable. A person is not a machine but a personality with the freedom and ability to choose. Theology is vigorous and biblical when it comes to grips with the hard facts of reality. Sin is reality. Sin and righteousness are poles apart. Righteousness and justice imply God's love, but the modern image of God has been marred by a sickly overemphasis on love.

Finally, a person is a sinner by practice. The Bible tells us that every person sins. "For all have sinned, and come short of the glory of God" (Rom. 3:23, KJV). "For the wages of sin is death; but the gift of God is eternal life" (Rom. 6:23, KJV).

Sin brings a sense of guilt. The guilt is toward God. Moral and legal guilt are not the same. Legal guilt relates to the group to which one belongs and the rules of that society. Moral guilt relates to a moral code or the hundreds of ethical systems. The Christian meaning of guilt is related to God. Paul spoke of the consequence of sin before God. Greater or lesser degrees of punishment are not taught in the Bible. Rather, for all sinners the ultimate outcome is the same—*death!*

The Gentiles were guilty and had incurred the wrath of God by resisting the truth of God (Rom. 1:18). They changed God's truth into a lie and exalted the creature more than the Creator (Rom. 1:25). The Jews were guilty because their faith had disintegrated into the legalistic outward form which exalted the law. They knew nothing of the spirit of the law of life. Paul taught, "For he is not a Jew, which is one outwardly; neither is that circumcision, which is outward in the flesh: But he is a Jew, which is one inwardly; and circumcision is that of the heart, in the spirit, and not in the letter; whose praise is not of men, but of God" (Rom. 2:28-29, KJV). Paul announced God's final verdict that the whole world is guilty before God (Rom. 3:9).

One of the major sins of Christians is the sin of omission. Any Christian who does not become a part of the redemptive mission of Christ will be a short circuit in the Christian movement. A great space missile may be destroyed or thrown completely off course by the malfunction of one little part. A few misdirected Christians can ground the current of spiritual power in God's church. A Christian is either a conductor of the power of God or a short circuit of the power of God. A Christian is an open road or a roadblock to the march of God's people in evangelizing.

The Remedy for Sin

The only remedy for sin is the death of Christ on the cross. Paul spoke with a burning conviction of the personal force of evil. He said that "we wrestle not against flesh and blood, but against principalities, against powers, against the rulers of the darkness of this world, against spiritual wickedness in high places" (Eph. 6:12, KJV).

If anyone whom the Holy Spirit is convicting of sin will turn and come to God and offer up by faith the death of Christ on the cross as a sacrifice for sins, that person will be liberated and given a nature no longer prone to sin. Evangelism comes to grip with sin and declares that Jesus is the answer. Evangelism urges sinners to accept Jesus Christ as Savior and Lord.

Salvation in Christ

In the Old Testament, "salvation" often referred to the deliverance of Israel from servitude to other nations. However, its primary meaning refers to the spiritual deliverance of God's people. "Salvation" in the New Testament sense is threefold. Three great theological words set it forth: regeneration, sanctification, and glorification.

Regeneration makes one a new creation in Christ.—When one has heard the gospel and chooses to accept it, that person has responded to the convicting work of the Spirit (1 Thess. 2:13-14). Conversion is turning toward God in repentance with faith in the Lord Jesus Christ. As one is thus converted, the Holy Spirit does His work of regeneration in the inner life of the man or woman. The convert becomes a new creation (2 Cor. 5:17) and experiences a new birth (John 3:3-8; Titus 3:4-5).

Salvation embraces more than the new birth.—In regeneration the believer's spirit is reborn. Sin is forgiven. One can truly say, "I have been saved." The penalty for sin is gone. However, the power of sin still remains in the convert's life. Sanctification is the process of being saved from the power of sin. Sanctification is the progressive maturity of the believer in keeping with the new nature received through the new birth (1 Thess. 4:3-8). It is the process of being transformed from the image of the world and conformed to the image of Christ (Rom. 8:29; 12:1-2). The new nature, which is the indwelling Spirit, enables one to live a life characterized by righteousness (Lev. 11:44).

Sanctification is not perfection, nor is sanctification entirely complete in this life. People often think that sanctification is a state of sinless living, void of any evil. That remains for the third stage of the New Testament concept of salvation, when one is freed from the presence of sin.

In glorification the body is redeemed from the dust and is changed into a body like the resurrection body of Jesus.—Jesus was the first fruits of those who slept (1 Cor. 15:20). At death, the spirit of a believer goes to be with God, but the body returns to the dust. When Jesus Christ returns, He will bring the spirit of each saved person with Him and the body shall be raised incorruptible and reunited with the spirit (1 Thess. 4:13-17; 1 Cor. 15:51-54). Therefore complete glorification means that the spirit is reunited with the body, and the body is changed from the dust to a spiritual or resurrection body. The Christian will be with God forever (1 Cor. 15:42-45). When one has been glorified, salvation is completed. Therefore, salvation is regeneration, sanctification, and glorification. It is redemption of the spirit, the physical life, and the body. When people are reborn and have received regeneration, they are made members of the body of Christ and should become members of a local church. Then it is essential that they grow in grace and develop into the kind of full-grown, effective Christians God designed them to be.

The Nature of the Church

We speak of the New Testament church here only as it is related to evangelism. In Acts, and indeed all through the New Testament, believers in Christ united with the church (Acts 2:47; 6:6; 9:31; Rom. 1:7; 1 Cor. 1:2). The Greek word for church in the New Testament is *ekklēsia*. Used 120 times in the New Testament, it refers to a local, called-out assembly of believers in Christ in all but three instances. The church constitutes a separate community within a community whose members are set apart from their neighbors by their faith, practice, and mutual affection for each other and for Jesus Christ.

The New Testament does not define "church," but it gives word pictures of it in action and points out its mission. From these pictures we learn about the nature of the church, and from its assigned task and nature we can define "church" (Eph. 4:3-16). The New Testament church is a fellowship of born-again, baptized believers in Christ, a company held together by the strong bonds of love for Christ and for each other. It is Christ-centered and Holy-Spirit-indwelt. If we leave out any of these statements, we do not have a clear definition of the church.

A local church is the basis of operation for New Testament evangelism. The redeemed person should be nurtured and developed in the church. Every believer should be baptized into the fellowship of the church and equipped to serve.

Motivation for Evangelism

Evangelism must be properly motivated. Evangelism has two true motives: love for Christ and the power of the Holy Ghost.

Jesus said the greatest commandment is, "Thou shalt love the Lord thy God with all thine heart, and with all thy soul, and with all thy might" (Deut. 6:5, KJV). And the second is like it: "Thou shalt love thy neighbour as thyself" (Lev. 19:18, KJV). Jesus also gave a new commandment on love: "A new commandment I give unto you, That ye love one another; as I have loved you, that ye also love one another" (John 13:34, KJV). If God's people love God better than anything or anyone, they will keep the first commandment. If they love their neighbors as well as they love themselves, they will keep the second commandment. If they love each other as much as Jesus loved them, they will be motivated to evangelize. Their lives will be in keeping with the love within them.

The Holy Spirit is the propelling motivation in evangelism. He is a burning, driving force within. After Pentecost the disciples could only choose to speak for Christ. They did not count the cost (Acts 4:13-20). They were not cautious for their own safety. Public opinion and threats from religious leaders did not matter. The Holy Spirit within them was bigger than themselves and the world around them; this thrust them onward (Acts 1:8; 2:4; 4:18-20; 29-31; 11:19-20; 13:2-4). After they were filled with the Holy Spirit, they began to witness from village to village, from province to province. They proclaimed Christ as the crucified, resurrected, redeeming Savior and Lord. They planted churches, suffered persecution, and were imprisoned and killed; but they were never hushed. Their message and methods would have been impotent without the motivation of love and the Holy Spirit.

Note

1. E. Y. Mullins, *The Christian Religion in Its Doctrinal Expression* (Nashville: The Sunday School Board, 1917), 2.

6 | The Holy Spirit in Evangelism
Charles L. Chaney

The participants in a consultation, sponsored by the Lausanne Committee for World Evangelization, convened in May, 1985. They prepared a summary statement of their conclusions:

> World evangelization is the central task of the Church. The Holy Spirit was poured out on the day of Pentecost to equip God's people for their global task, and today the same Spirit renews his people and thrusts them into mission. Through repentance, faith, and receiving the fullness of the Spirit, we are renewed. In obedience to the inspired Word of God and under guidance of the Holy Spirit, we, therefore, are called into costly discipleship as individuals, families, and churches. The task of world evangelization can only be carried out by people who are open to the Spirit, and whose lives are transformed by his power.[1]

This paragraph could serve as a text for a paper on the place and function of the Holy Spirit in evangelism. I want, however, to place this fresh statement in the background and turn to a more basic text: the words of Jesus and their context in the opening paragraphs of Acts.

> And gathering them together, He commanded them not to leave Jerusalem, but to wait for what the Father had promised, "Which," He said, "you heard of from Me; for John baptized with water, but you shall be baptized with the Holy Spirit not many days from

55

now." And so when they had come together, they were asking Him, saying, "Lord, is it at this time You are restoring the kingdom of Israel?" He said to them, "It is not for you to know times or epochs which the Father has fixed by His own authority; but you shall receive power when the Holy Spirit has come upon you; and you shall be My witnesses both in Jerusalem, and all Judea and Samaria, and even to the remotest part of the earth" (Acts 1:4-8 NASB).[2]

The Spirit Promised

This rendezvous was planned. At least 120 disciples gathered from Galilee, Judea, Jerusalem, and its vicinity. They ate together, as in a big family reunion. They recalled and discussed the events of the past 42 months. They asked questions, trying to gain understanding. Primarily they listened in wonder to Jesus' last words.

Jesus took them back to the beginning of the good news, to the days of John the Baptist. He reminded them of the promise of the Father. He announced its imminent fulfillment. Three significant elements compose this extended paragraph in Acts.

A Baffling Command and Its Explanation (Acts 1:4-5)

Jesus commanded His followers to wait. They were to remain in Jerusalem until the promise of the Father became a reality. He explained exactly what the promise was. Just as John submerged his disciples in water, the disciples of Jesus were to be submerged in the Holy Spirit.

A Burning Question and Its Answer (Acts 1:6-7)

Once again, the question of timing surfaced. Jesus dealt with it again, with infinite patience. This was the great question that devout Jews had been asking since the end of the Maccabean period at least, and probably since the fall of Jerusalem in 586 B.C. Jesus' answer was simple and direct: some things the Father has fixed by His own authority and has chosen not to reveal them to humans. In spite of Jesus' answer, some disciples, in every age since Jesus spoke, have tried to prove Him wrong.

A Bold Announcement and Its Consequence (Acts 1:8)

After receiving the gift that the Father had promised, Jesus told them, they would receive power. As a result, they would be His witnesses in Jerusalem, then in all Judea and Samaria, and in the most remote part of the earth. Like ripples that rush in all directions from a stone dropped in a pond, wherever, whenever, and for whatever reason the disciples may go, they would be His witnesses. An understanding of this biblical passage is fundamental to an understanding of the role of the Holy Spirit in evangelism.

The Promise of the Father

What was this "promise of the Father"? Its fulfillment came ten days later at the feast of Pentecost. Several Old Testament passages provide keys to understanding what Jesus meant by these words.

The Marks of a New Era

The most obvious reference is Joel 2:28-32, which contains the promise that in the last days God would pour out His Spirit on mankind. The salient characteristics of the new era are described in detail.

First, it would be an age of *extraordinary spiritual vision*; a time when inspired, redeemed imagination would combine with undaunted faith to attempt God-given dreams (Acts 2:17-18). God would pour out His Spirit on "ALL MANKIND." Old and young alike, both men and women, would be shot through with the global vision of the risen Christ. They would dream impossible dreams and see unimaginable visions of the expansion of God's kingdom and the growth of the church among all peoples. Jesus taught that the Holy Spirit is the author of such spiritual vision, for He would take what was uniquely Jesus Christ's and make it known to Christ's disciples (John 16:14-15).

Second, this distinctive age of the Holy Spirit's work would be marked by a *universal call to ministry* given to all the servants of God (Acts 2:18). The Spirit of God would be poured out on all His servants, male and female; not for just a few select prophets, as in the Old Testament era. All would prophesy. In these latter days, all God's servants have received His Spirit, and all are called to a God-given ministry.

The third mark of the age of the Holy Spirit would be a *combination of amazing feats of human achievement, repeated and enormous natural calamities, and immense social problems* (Acts 2:19-20). God's calling of His people may be done in times of extreme stress and with inordinate difficulty, even in the midst of astonishing human progress.

Fourth, this new age would be marked by a *universal offer of salvation*. "Everyone who calls on the name of the Lord shall be saved" (Acts 2:21, NASB). The outpouring of the Holy Spirit on the day of Pentecost was, in a fashion, the birth of the evangelistic task of the church.

Evangelism took place in the ministry of Jesus, in the ministry of John the Baptist, and even in the era of the patriarchs and prophets. Evangelism was a reality then, but became more illuminated when Jesus had finished His work, had been exalted to the Father's right hand, and "having received from the Father the promise of the Holy Spirit," had poured Him forth (Acts 2:33, NASB). "Pentecost is a new beginning—the inauguration of the new age, the age of the Spirit—that which had not been before."[3] After Pentecost, evangelism became, in a new and far more dramatic way, the task of the church. "The preaching of the gospel is the central task entrusted to the church in the period called 'the last days.'"[4]

The boundaries of the last days are marked by the ascension of Jesus; and the outpouring of the Spirit on the one side, and the return of Jesus from heaven on the other (Acts 1:11). The latter event waits on the completion of the evangelistic task. "And this gospel of the kingdom will be preached in the whole world as a testimony to all nations, and then the end will come" (Matt. 24:14). We still live in the last days; in the time of the outpouring of the Holy Spirit, in the age of the apostles. The same distinctive marks identified by Joel and Peter characterize our own age.

The faithful execution of the evangelistic task gives substance and consistency to the history of our own era. "It is the ... reality underlying ... secular history."[5] Evangelism results in the progressive building-up of the body of Christ. This process is principally the work of the Holy Spirit, carried out through the churches. Since the execution of the evangelistic task is what gives meaning to history, evangelism must be the major priority of the churches.

The Mediation of a New Heart

The "promise of the Father" refers to a recurring theme in Ezekiel 36—39, expressed succinctly in 36:25-27.

> I will sprinkle clean water on you, and you will be clean; I will
> cleanse you from all your impurities and from all your idols. I will

give you a new heart and put a new spirit in you; I will remove from
you your heart of stone and give you a heart of flesh. And I will put
my Spirit in you and move you to follow my decrees and be careful
to keep my laws.

The work of the Messiah was twofold: to cleanse people from
sin (forgiveness) and to implant a new heart within them (regeneration). The purpose of Christ's coming is described in the same
way in all the gospels. The best illustration is the Baptist's witness to Jesus. John identified Jesus as "the Lamb of God who
takes away the sin of the world" (John 1:29). "He who sent me to
baptize in water," He continued, "said to me, 'He upon whom you
see the Spirit descending and remaining... this is the one who
baptizes in the Holy Spirit.' And I have seen... this is the Son of
God" (John 1:33-34, NASB).

Jesus Christ came not only to cleanse but also to impart new
life. He bestows the gift of God's Spirit. The cleansing was
achieved by His death and verified by His resurrection. The gift of
the Spirit was made possible by His exaltation and confirmed by
the events of Pentecost. "Having been exalted to the right hand of
God, and having received from the Father the promise of the Holy
Spirit, He has poured forth this which you both see and hear"
(Acts 2:33, NASB). "The characteristic work of Jesus is twofold,"
John Stott says. "It involves a removal and a bestowal, a taking
away of sin and a baptizing (in) the Holy Spirit. These are the two
great gifts of Jesus Christ".[6]

The testimony of John the Baptist, reported in all four gospels,
makes it clear that baptism in the Holy Spirit is something Jesus
does. The Holy Spirit is the sphere into which the disciple is
baptized. The word used in reference to the baptism that Jesus
administers is better translated "in,"[7] rather than "with" in the
English New Testament. The One coming after John, whom John
clearly identified as Jesus of Nazareth, was to "baptize in the
Holy Spirit" (Matt. 3:11; Mark 1:8; Luke 3:16). The baptism in the
Holy Spirit is a ministry performed by the Son.[8]

The outpouring of the Holy Spirit marked the long-awaited day
when God would dwell within his people as individuals, giving
them a new spirit, the Spirit of God Himself. Before Pentecost,
the Spirit had only been with God's people. He had anointed and
equipped individuals for service.[9] Since Pentecost, He has also
taken up residence in them.

Not all the devout men and women of Israel (like Zechariah,

Simeon, and Anna), not all the converts of John the Baptist (Acts 9:1-7), and not all the disciples of Jesus were in Jerusalem on the day of Pentecost. They had repented, and, like all devout believers of the Old Testament, they had received the forgiveness of sins in anticipation of the coming of the Messiah. They were justified by their faith. They had not received a new heart. The hiatus between the outpouring of the Spirit and that divine fact being communicated to devout men and women over the Roman world explains the disjunction in the book of Acts at times between the act of repentance and faith and the reception of the Holy Spirit. After Pentecost, the promise of the Father had to be told to all those disciples and devout Israelites.

The pattern today, however, is that of Cornelius and his household. While Peter was preaching the forgiveness of sins by faith in Jesus Christ, these Gentiles received the gift of the Spirit. When they believed, they were submerged in the Holy Spirit, without the laying on of hands and before water baptism (Acts 10:43-48), They received the same gift that the 120 disciples and 3,000 converts had received at Pentecost. The Spirit took up His dwelling place in their bodies. In fact, the reception of the Spirit became the basis for receiving water baptism. Peter explained to the apostles and elders that "the Holy Spirit fell upon them, just as He did upon us at the beginning...If God therefore gave to them the same gift as He gave to us also after believing in the Lord Jesus Christ, who was I that I could stand in God's way?" (Acts 11:15, 17, NASB). Evidence that one has received the gift of the Spirit remains the grounds for water baptism today. Writing a generation later than Luke, John explained that when Jesus promised rivers of living water flowing from his disciples to others, he "spoke of the Spirit, whom those who believed in Him were to receive; for the Spirit was not yet given, because Jesus was not yet glorified" (John 7:38-39, NASB). What was "not yet" became a reality on the day of Pentecost. "Therefore if any man is in Christ, he is a new creature; the old things passed away, behold, new things have come" (2 Cor. 5:17, NASB). The Holy Spirit is integrally related to evangelism through regeneration, the bestowal of a new heart, and a new spirit. The Holy Spirit Himself is that new spirit in all regenerated persons.

The Mobilization of the New Israel

Jesus spent more than three years raising up His new temple. He erected a new dwelling place for God. The Holy Spirit was poured out to dwell in that new temple, which was one not made with stone and wood but built with living stones—forgiven and regenerated disciples. After Pentecost, God no longer dwelt with His people through tabernacles and edifices; God now dwells *in* His people, the body of Christ, the new Israel.

When one receives the gift of the Spirit, he is added to the body of Christ. The primary purpose of baptism in the Holy Spirit is to make all believers members of one another and of Christ. Those in Christ are "no longer foreigners and aliens, but you are fellow citizens with the saints and are of God's household . . . being built together to become a dwelling of God in the Spirit" (Eph. 2:19, 22 NASB). This foremost purpose of incorporation into Christ's body is stated emphatically in 1 Corinthians 12:12-13.

> For even as the body is one and yet has many members, and all the members of the body, through they are many, are one body, so also is Christ. For [in] one Spirit we were all baptized into one body, whether Jews or Greeks, whether slaves or free, and we were all made to drink of one Spirit (NASB, alt. rdg.).

"Therefore, the purpose of the baptism (in) the Holy Spirit is to incorporate the believer into the body of Christ."[10]

At Pentecost, Peter did not address the gathered pilgrims as Jews, or even as sons of Jacob. He deliberately used the covenant designation of the people of God, "Men of Israel." In fact, the promise in Joel was not to all the descendants of Abraham or Jacob. The promise was to the remnant, to the little flock. From the beginning, the primitive Christians regarded themselves as the true Israel. "They were the Church or People of God. They did not separate from Israel. . . . It was the rebellious sons of Israel who forfeited their covenant by rejecting Christ."[11] Not only did the true Israel have claim to all the promises of God, but also to all the responsibility of blessing the nations. The evangelistic effectiveness of the early church did not arise simply out of obedience to the external command contained in the Great Commission of Jesus. It was expressive rather of an urge that had its roots in the new spiritual life imparted by the gift of the Holy Spirit. At Pentecost the Holy Spirit made the church, as the body of Christ, His dwelling place. In that act, the church became a witnessing community. The evangelistic witness of the church began at the precise moment of the descent of the Spirit. The church is, first and last, a witnessing, proclaiming, evangelistic community.

The tasks of this community is made clear by the contrast between the New Testament *ekklēsia* and the Old Testament *kahal* (congregation). Until Pentecost, the central place of meeting had been a temple; the primary religious leader, a priest; the principle cultic instrument, the altar; and the salient cultic act, the sacrifice. After Pentecost the cultic system was abrogated. Instead, the preaching of the gospel and the ongoing observance of baptism and the Lord's Supper were the customary procedures. At Pentecost a new community, intentionally gathered by Jesus, was energized. The Old Testament *kahal* gave way to the evangelizing *ekklēsia* of the New Testament.[12]

The temple was now composed of the people of God, who were filled by the Spirit of God. They, and all who would join them, constituted a new humanity in Christ, and they are "like living stones ... being built into a spiritual house to be a holy priesthood, offering spiritual sacrifices acceptable to God through Jesus Christ" (1 Pet. 2:5). The Spirit, indwelling a temple of living men and women, created a community that was by nature a witnessing body. They were "a chosen people, a royal priesthood, a holy nation, a people belonging to God, that ... declare the praises of him who called [them] out of darkness into his wonderful light" (1 Pet. 2:9).

The evangelistic commissions of Jesus are not only commands to be obeyed, but also the law that expresses the nature and governs the life of the churches. "The outpouring of the Spirit is in and by reason of its very nature the effectuation of the Great Commission in the life of the church."[13] The Spirit has been given also to local fellowships of believers. Since the Spirit dwells in them, these churches are, by nature, evangelistic. The Spirit indwells the churches, and each regenerated member is by nature a witness. "The *Whole Church*, therefore, is a witnessing Church, whether officially and corporately ... or through her members personally and individually."[14] At Pentecost the church became an evangelistic organism because the indwelling Spirit made Christ's evangelistic mandate an organic part of the church's being.[15]

The Power of the Spirit

Jesus not only assured His disciples that they would be baptized in the Spirit, He also averred that, when it happened, they would be empowered by the Spirit and become His witnesses. Jesus' words intimate that the Spirit's power would enable them to witness so effectively that people would follow Jesus from every corner of the earth. "The mission of the Holy Spirit," J.B. Lawrence said, "is the evangelization of the world."[16]

The Events of Pentecost

From the perspective of the 120 disciples, four separate events took place at Pentecost. First *Old Testament prophecy was fulfilled.* Pentecost was one of seven great feasts of Israel. All seven feasts were fulfilled in the life, death, resurrection and ascension of Jesus.[17] Pentecost was no after-thought of God, nor was what happened that day ultimately the result of ten days of confession and prayer. The outpouring of the Holy Spirit was part of the eternal purpose and plan of God.

Second, *three extraordinary, observable manifestations of the Spirit's presence took place.* The rushing wind, the tongues of fire, and the ability to praise God in languages never learned may have been repeated in other times and places, but no biblical record exists of the reoccurrence. There is evidence of ecstatic languages in the Corinthian church. However, Paul's statement that they must be accompanied by interpretation sets that phenomena apart from what happened at Pentecost. No interpreter was needed for the Jewish pilgrims to understand the praises of God in their own languages.

Third, already discussed at length, *the gathered church was submerged in the Holy Spirit.* The Spirit of God was poured out, and all the disciples were made to drink of that one Spirit (1 Cor. 12:13).

Fourth, *the gathered church, and each individual member of it, was filled with the Holy Spirit.* The distinction between the "baptism in" and "fullness of" the Holy Spirit is most critical. Much of the turmoil among Christians today about the Holy Spirit results from puzzlement about these two distinct aspects of the believer's relationship to Him.

The Fullness of the Spirit

The *baptism* in the Spirit is a work of the Son of God. Occurring only once in believers' lives, when they are regenerated, this benchmark is established when God's Spirit comes to dwell in the believer. Its purpose is to make the believer a living, functioning member of the body of Christ.

The *filling* of the Spirit is something that the Spirit does after He takes up His residence in the believer. This milestone in one's life is reached when the Holy Spirit, who already indwells, is permitted to control that believer's life. Its purpose is an endowment of supernatural power for effective testimony to Christ.

When one is filled with the Spirit, he allows the Spirit, who is a resident in his life, to become the president of his life. The Spirit's filling may occur many times. In Acts, believers were filled with the Spirit on various occasions (Acts 2:4; 4:8,31; 6:3,5; 7:55; 9:17; 13:9,52). The Spirit's fullness must be appropriated every day, challenge by challenge, moment by moment.

All believers can be filled with the Spirit and walk in the Spirit's power because they have received the gift of the Spirit. The Spirit's fullness is not just for the apostles and prophets, or other super Christians. At Pentecost, the entire church was filled with the Holy Spirit (Acts 2:4). Pentecost was, in fact, a demonstration of such infinite power that it is immeasurable. It enabled disciples of Jesus to transform lives and change the course of history. That power is available today to enable believers to live holy and fruitful lives. Every Christian is privileged and commanded to be filled with God's Spirit and permit Him to empower his life.[18]

The Role of the Spirit

Four questions will bring the Spirit's role in evangelism into focus.

Why Does the Spirit Fill Believers?

Jesus' words in Acts 1:8 connect the filling of the Spirit incontrovertibly with the evangelistic task. R. A. Torrey, in his final book, asserted that the Spirit's filling is "always connected with and primarily for the purpose of testimony and service." He insisted that there is "not one single passage in the Bible ... where (the Spirit's fullness) is not connected with testimony or service."[19]

If this statement is true, the primary purpose of the fullness of the Spirit is *not* to make the believer individually holy, or to make him personally happy. The **purpose** of the Spirit's fullness is to make one useful to God in the salvation of souls. Sanctification is certainly a work of the Spirit, and part of the fruit the Spirit bears in the life of the believer is joy. Nevertheless, the primary reason that the Holy Spirit fills believers is to enable them to bear effective testimony to Christ. Spiritual "highs" are important, and holy living is essential to the Christian life. However, wave after wave of unsaved men, women, and children are sweeping to a hopeless eternity. Better to spend one's life without spiritual thrills and have power to reach some of these people for Christ than to have repeated ecstasies and be unable to turn men and women to Christ.[20]

The Spirit, Jesus said, "shall glorify Me; for He shall take of Mine, and shall disclose it to you" (John 16:14, NASB). The Holy Spirit magnifies Christ by making Him known.[21] This He does chiefly through the witness of Spirit-filled disciples. The two paramount modes of effective witness are a victorious life and an anointed ministry. In the first, the believer reigns over the circumstances and troubles of life in a manner that attracts people to Christ. In the second, the believer exercises his gifts and performs his God-given ministry in a manner that leads people to turn to Christ. Both are the result of being filled with the Spirit.

What Conditions Are Prerequisite to the Filling of the Spirit?

Repentance from sin and faith in Jesus Christ are the only conditions required before one receives the gift of the Spirit.[22] That is the most prevalent pattern in Acts and is the general teaching of the New Testament regarding the reception of the Holy Spirit (Gal. 3:2, 14, 4:6; Rom. 5:5, 8:9, 14-16).[23] But the believer is not necessarily filled with God's Spirit from the moment he becomes a disciple. In fact, most believers first experience the fullness of the Spirit after they have been followers of Christ for several years. When a new believer is immediately filled with the Spirit, it is because certain spiritual conditions are present in his life at the time.

Five statements can be made that describe the spiritual conditions that existed in the lives of the 120 believers when they were filled with the Spirit.[24]

These disciples had forsaken everything for Christ.—Their allegiance to Christ was no longer in question. The words of Jesus had been remembered and believed, "Any of you who does not give up everything he has cannot be my disciple" (Luke 14:33, NIV). This was the first step in their preparation for being filled with the Spirit.

These believers had been brought to utter self-despair and honesty.—The ten days between ascension and Pentecost were spent in self-examination, confession of sin, and getting right with one another, as well as in prayer. Before Jesus' crucifixion, His apostles had made bold boasts of loyalty and love. By the day of Pentecost, they were at the end of themselves, having no confidence in their own resolution or their ability to perform in their own strength. They had come to true brokenness.

The 120 disciples had an intense, personal attachment to Jesus Christ.—They loved Jesus with their feelings, minds, and wills. This had not always been true. Their love for Jesus had been exceedingly shallow. By the day of Pentecost, these men and women were clinging to Jesus with intense and unbroken devotion and love.

These believers received by faith Jesus' promise to clothe them with supernatural power.—They took Jesus at His word. They waited; they waited; they waited. They did not understand it all, but they did believe Him. Jesus had said that they would be empowered to witness; they adhered to that word.

These disciples hungered and thirsted to receive the fullness of the Spirit.—They not only waited; but they also prayed. They would not be satisfied with anything less than what Jesus had promised.

All these factors were prerequisite to being filled with the Spirit in the first century. They are also prerequisite to being filled with the Spirit today.

What Are the Evidences of the Spirit's Fullness?

Numerous opinions and myths circulate today about what constitutes proof of the Spirit's fullness. Some of these opinions offer inconclusive evidence of the Spirit's fullness.

Inconclusive evidence.—(1) The absence of trouble and the presence of unmitigated happiness in not conclusive proof that one is filled with the Spirit of God. Jesus was full of the Holy Spirit and was led by the Spirit into the wilderness to be tempted by the devil (Luke 4:1). Gethsemane was hardly unmitigated happiness. In fact, acting in the Spirit's fullness often propels people into conflict with the flesh, the world, and the devil.[25] One filled with the Spirit defies the flesh, the old Adamic nature. Similarly, he withstands the world, a term which encompasses the whole circle of material goods and pleasures, and the social, political, and economic systems that control people and seduce them away from God. He also resists the devil and his demonic forces operating in the universe. Stephen was filled with the Spirit (Acts 6:5), and it resulted in his death.

(2) Mind-boggling success with growing influence or control over material and human resources is not incontrovertible evidence that one is filled with the Spirit. Since the principal purpose of the Spirit's filling is an effective evangelistic witness to Christ, such success is contradictory. Walking in the power of God's Spirit often enables a disciple to launch a movement that impacts thousands of people, produces material resources, and creates ongoing institutions. However, other forces can and do produce the same results. Very often when an individual or a group of individuals in the power of the Spirit do come into control of human and physical resources, they discover the "corruption that is in the world by lust" at work (2 Pet. 1:4, NASB).

Power and success tend to corrupt. All that can be encompassed under the term *lust*, inflames rapacious ambition, and spurs in us the pride of life, are part of the Satanic system. Everything that fires the furnace of pride is of the world. Eminence, riches, accomplishment—these are extolled by the world. Humans may be justly proud of success, but that which brings this success may be of the world.

> Every success therefore that we experience (and I am not suggesting that we should be failures!) calls in us for an instant, humble confession of its inherent sinfulness, for whenever we meet success we have in some degree touched the world-system.[26]

Instead of providing proof that one is filled with the Spirit, numerical success and the accumulation of material resources may lead to the Spirit's being grieved or quenched.

(3) The manifestation of extraordinary wonders and miraculous gifts (even speaking in ecstatic tongues) is not indisputable evidence of the Spirit's fullness. The Pentecostal movement has been used widely around the world to advance the cause of Christ in this century. Classical Pentecostal doctrine alleges that the evidence that one has received the *baptism of the Spirit* is to speak in ecstatic tongues. Although this experience is not precisely the same for Pentecostals as the *filling of the Spirit*, for most there would be a close association between having manifested the *sign* of tongues (as distinguished from the *gift* of tongues) and the power to have an effective ministry. This view cannot be sustained by Scripture. There are only three alleged examples of the sign of tongues: Acts 2:4, 10:45-46, and 19:6. All these examples can better be explained as something other than

the sign of tongues. There is no reference in the doctrinal sections of the Bible to the sign of tongues.

In America today, and especially in some cultures around the world where the church is growing rapidly, there is a head-to-head clash between the kingdom of God and the kingdom of Satan. Many reports and hard evidence of the miraculous intervention of God in the lives of men and women exists. Such power encounters are inevitable. They have been happening throughout the history of Christianity, and are to be expected where the church is confronting the kingdom of evil. Spiritual warfare does not take place unless God's people are ministering in the Holy Spirit's fullness and power. Nevertheless, signs, wonders, and miraculous gifts do not necessarily indicate that one is filled with the Spirit. Even Satan masqueraded as an angel of light (2 Cor. 11:13-14), and some of those who do these things may not even know Christ (Matt. 7:21-23).

Irrefutable evidence.—What then does give irrefutable evidence of the Spirit's fullness?[27] (1) When one is filled with the Holy Spirit *the continual presence of Jesus is realized in his life.* Christ promised to bestow the gift of the Spirit to those who believe on Him. On the night of His arrest He told His disciples that He would live in them in an abiding spiritual presence (John 14:15-21). A divine inflow of life, supernatural in quality, would be followed by a divine outflow of life, supernatural in power (John 14:23-26; 15:1-5). He promised that power for such a life would come from "another Comforter" who would take up permanent residence in them.

On the day of Pentecost, Christ fulfilled His promise and poured out the Spirit. Since that event, everyone who has been organically and vitally united by faith with the risen Christ has received the gift of the Spirit (Acts 11:15,17). From the moment one receives Jesus Christ, that believer is *in* the Spirit and the Spirit is *in* him. "It is impossible to accept the Son and to refuse the Spirit."[28] For "you are not in the flesh but in the Spirit, if indeed the Spirit of God dwells in you. But if anyone does not have the Spirit of Christ, he does not belong to Him" (Rom. 8:9, NASB).

Nevertheless, many contemporary believers live as though they were all alone. Christ lives within them, but He is there unnoticed. God's purpose is that every believer would live a life marked by a deep, growing spirituality and exercise a ministry marked by a flowing, supernatural effectiveness. Abundant life is every believer's birthright; not the privilege of a few but the prerogative of all. The abiding presence of Jesus is fully realized in a believer's life only when one is filled with the Spirit.

(2) When one is filled with the Spirit **the holy life of Jesus is reproduced in the believer's life**. Not a veneer, not a simulation, but the demonstrable evidence of holy love flowing out to others is the sign of the Spirit's fullness. "But the fruit of the Spirit is love, joy, peace, patience, kindness, goodness, faithfulness, gentleness, and self-control" (Gal. 5:22-23, NASB). The fruit of the Spirit is the character and beauty of Jesus manifested in the life of the believer. Paul described this graphically when he said:

> We have this treasure in jars of clay to show that this all-surpassing power is from God and not from us. We are hard pressed on every side, but not crushed; perplexed, but not in despair; persecuted, but not abandoned; struck-down, but not destroyed. We always carry around in our body the death of Jesus, so that the life of Jesus may also be revealed in our body. For we who are alive are always being given over to death for Jesus' sake, so that his life may be revealed in our mortal body (2 Cor. 4:7-11).

Jesus Christ wants to do far more in the life of the believer than help him live a holy life. The risen Christ wants to live His life anew and afresh in the mortal body of the believer. Christ wants the believer's hands to be His hands; the believer's feet to be His feet; the believer's mouth to be His mouth; the believer's mind to be His mind. He wants to duplicate His holy life in the believer's life.

When the Spirit fills one's life, He does not negate nor obliterate the personality and distinctiveness of the believer. The believer is never so unique, so genuine, so real as when he permits the Spirit of God to fill him and manifest the character and disposition of Jesus in his life. Paul said, "I have been crucified with Christ; and it is no longer I who live, but Christ lives in me; and the life which I now live in the flesh I live by faith in the Son of God, who loved me and delivered Himself up for me" (Gal. 2:20, NASB).

(3) When one is filled with the Holy Spirit *the mighty works of Jesus are re-enacted in that believer's life*. Jesus' strange and disturbing words in John 14:12 are almost offensive to modern evangelicals: "Truly, truly, I say to you, he who believes in Me, the works that I do shall he do also; and greater works than these shall he do; because I go to the Father" (NASB). Many modern

disciples, though intent on serving Christ, do not know how to take these words.

This saying of Christ has been interpreted four ways: 1) some insist that Jesus did not say these words; they were created by a penmen and put into the mouth of Jesus; 2) some suggest that Jesus was mistaken; 3) some assert that Jesus was speaking of miracles; and 4) some allege that Jesus was not speaking of supernatural feats, but of another genre of works, more significant than wonder-producing signs. Individuals within this group differ with one another about whether miraculous deeds happen today.[29]

Acts reveals that miracles of Jesus did continue in the ministry of His followers. The thrust of Acts is found in the things Jesus began to do and teach in the days of His flesh and continued to do through His Spirit-filled disciples (Acts 2:4). However, this statement must be qualified. No evidence exists that all, or even most, of the followers of Jesus healed or cast out demons. No evidence exists that those who did perform miracles performed them all the time. Phillip was not transported around to all of his appointments. At times he had to walk or ride a mule. It must also be said, however, that such expressions of the Holy Spirit's power were not confined to the apostles. Ordinary laymen were sometimes involved. Phillip and Stephen are primary examples.

The context of Jesus' word about "greater works" was full of detail about the coming of the Spirit. As a result of that coming, Jesus promised, "He who believes in Me, the works that I do shall he do also" (John 14:12, NASB). Unquestionably this refers to His miracles, but I believe Jesus was speaking of much more. When Jesus said "the works that I do shall he do also," He was referring to the miracles that He Himself performed. Throughout Christian history certain men and women have had ministries marked by the miraculous. Has anyone, however, ever performed miracles greater in scope than those of Jesus? What miracles could be greater than restoring sight, raising the dead, or calming storms? When Jesus went on to say, "And greater works than these shall he do," He was speaking of an entirely different sort of works. He was speaking of works greater in significance and importance. Instead of manifestations of physical change, He was speaking of spiritual accomplishments. "Anything done to the spirit of man is far more significant than something done to the body. That is what Jesus is speaking of."[30]

Jesus spoke of the enormous spread of Christianity, the great work of world evangelization. When one is filled with the Spirit—whatever his spiritual gifts—he is used by God to testify about Jesus Christ and becomes an instrument of the evangelistic mandate. This re-enactment of these mighty works of Jesus, whether accompanied by miraculous signs in one's ministry or not, is evidence of the Spirit's fullness in one's life.

How Does One Experience the Power of the Spirit?

Paul's instructions to the Asian Christians are very explicit. "Do not get drunk on wine, which leads to debauchery. Instead, be filled with the Spirit" (Eph. 5:18, NIV). "Be filled with the Spirit" is in a Greek tense meaning "always be filled with the Spirit." The charge directs us constantly to be "clothed with power from on high" (Luke 24:49, NIV). Paul taught first-century believers, "Those who belong to Christ Jesus have crucified the sinful nature with its passions and desires. Since we live by the Spirit, let us keep in step with the Spirit" (Gal. 5:24-25, NIV).

Holy desperation summarizes the preconditions for the Spirit's fullness. This is not despair, depression, or self-deprecation. Rather, it is the God-given desire to be all, and have all, that Jesus intended for us in His service. The disciples of Jesus before Pentecost were riveted to Jerusalem by a hunger to have what the Father had promised. Jesus probably repeated many times in His ministry, "Blessed are those who hunger and thirst for righteousness, for they will be filled" (Matt. 5:6, NIV; see Luke 6:21). His dramatic words at the climax of the feast of tabernacles burned in their ears. "If any man is thirsty, let him come to Me and drink" (John 7:37, NASB). The fullness of the outpoured, indwelling Spirit comes only to those who will be satisfied with nothing less.

Holy desperation also expresses itself in radical honesty about what we do and what we are. Honesty about what we do—the *works* of the flesh—always results in humble confession and, where necessary, specific restitution. Perceived advantage in harboring hidden and unconfessed sins, for any reason, pales before the desire to be clothed in God's power. Honesty about what we are—the works of the *flesh*—always results in contrition and brokenness. Confidence in the energetic productivity of natural talents is exploded by radical honesty. Trust in gargantuan labors evaporates before truthfulness about the corruption of the old nature. One who will be filled with the Holy Spirit has an assiduously held conviction that "nothing good lives in me, that is, in my sinful nature" (Rom 7:18, NIV), and that Jesus' words are literally true "apart from me you can do nothing" (John 15:5, NIV). Only by coming to the end of self and by being desperate to have what God has intended for all His children, will you be filled with God's Spirit.

There are three keys to walking constantly in the Spirit's fullness.—(1) Full surrender. When you became a Christian, the Spirit of God came into your life to live in you until death or until the return of Christ unites you forever with Him. You received a new nature, a divine life. The Holy Spirit took up His abode in you. The old, fallen nature received from Adam has not been destroyed. The Bible exhorts us to be victorious over that old nature. It is still at work in our members. We now have two natures, the old man and the new man struggling within us. Therefore, Paul wrote,

> Live by the Spirit, and you will not gratify the desires of the sinful nature. For the sinful nature desires what is contrary to the Spirit, and the Spirit what is contrary to the sinful nature. They are in conflict with each other, so that you do not do what you want (Gal. 5:16-17, NIV).

Since the two natures are deadly foes, they struggle for the mastery of our lives. The old nature and the new nature want, not only, to be *in* us, but *to have full control* of us. Each one wants to fill us. The question is not "How shall I receive the Spirit?" The question now is, "Having two natures, how shall I be filled with *one* of them?" How are you to know the full and abundant life of the Spirit and be delivered from the life and power of your carnal nature?

James McConkey asserted:

> The answer of reason, revelation, and experience is the *absolute unqualified surrender of our life to God, to do His will instead of our own.* Thus, when we surrender our *sins* and believe, we *receive* the Holy Spirit; when we surrender our *lives* and believe, we are *filled* with the Holy Spirit. *Receiving* the Spirit is God's answer to repentance and faith; the *fullness* of the Spirit is God's answer to *surrender* and *faith.* At *conversion*, the Spirit enters; at *surrender* the Spirit, *already entered*, takes *full possession*. The supreme, human condition of the fullness of the Spirit is a life *wholly surrendered to God* to do His will.[31]

How do you make an absolute, unqualified surrender of your life to God? (a) Deliberately and consciously deny the claims and demands of the old nature (Eph. 4:22; Col. 3:5-8; Rom. 6:12). (b) Change your attitude of mind. Redirect the way you think. Rejoice in the victory that you have in Christ, because He has been triumphant in His death and resurrection over the penalty and power of sin. Count yourself part of that victory (Eph. 4:23; Col. 3:1-3; Rom. 6:9,11). (c) Yield your whole life, body, soul, and spirit to God to be clothed in your new nature. Intentionally give yourself to Him, without reserve. Make yourself the bondslave of Christ. Consciously make Him your Lord in every decision, act, and thought (Eph. 4:24; Col. 3:9-10; Rom. 6:13).

In comparing these Biblical references, I am not talking about three separate steps to full surrender. All three are one great act by which you make Jesus Christ Lord of all of your life. Paul summarized all of this in Romans 12:1-2.

(2) Simple faith. The second key to experiencing the Spirit's fullness is a simple, active faith that takes God at His word. By "simple faith," I mean the same measure of faith that enabled you to receive Jesus Christ as Savior and Lord and to become His disciple. This should not be confused with the faith that is the special gift of the Holy Spirit (1 Cor. 12:9) or the mature faith of one who has walked long with Jesus Christ. Any true disciple of Jesus already has all the faith that is needed.

The will of God is very clear in this matter. The words of Paul are a plain command. "Do not get drunk with wine ... but be filled with the Spirit" (Eph. 5:18, NASB). Drunkness can never be the good, pleasing, or perfect will of God for the believer, nor living a powerless, defeated, unfruitful life. Jesus said, "I have come that they may have life, and have it to the full" (John 10:10b). The Bible is plain. God's will is for His children to appropriate for themselves everything He has provided for them in Christ (2 Pet. 1:3-4). That appropriation is done *by faith* (1 John 5:14-15) Therefore, every one of us should act upon the need of his life and the promise of God. As you surrender your life totally to God, ask the Holy Spirit to fill your life with Himself.[32]

As you take this step, remember:

• Do not expect a great rapturous experience. Sometimes great joy, an overwhelming sense of peace, or waves of selfless love do sweep over you when you are filled with the Spirit—but not always and not often. These are emotions. They may come after the fact of being filled, but never before the fact. For most of us, it is a quiet time of timorous surrender and timid faith reaching out to claim what already belongs to us.

• Don't look for something from without to come in. You already have the Spirit dwelling in you. When you are filled with the Spirit, you are giving Him free reign in every nook and corner of your life. He must have the key to every room in your life, no matter how small. Nevertheless, He already dwells there. He is not *coming in*, but *filling up*.[33]

• Don't ignore the pre-conditions. No one is filled with the Spirit by much holy living and much prayer. You appropriate the Spirit by faith. Yet God's Spirit does not fill a vessel that is already filled with the old nature. If you still have confidence that all God's tasks can be done with your own natural abilities, well-honed skills, winsome personality, or boundless dedication, don't expect to be filled. You can't dedicate the old nature to God. It must be laid aside, denied, and mortified.

• Ask the Holy Spirit Himself to fill you. Don't say, "Lord, I'd like to be filled," or "Lord, I hope to be filled," or "Lord, help me to be filled." Say rather, "Holy Spirit of God, Who dwells constantly within me, I am powerless to do Your work in my own strength or by my own abilities. Please take full control of my life. Fill me now."

• Thank Him for hearing your prayer and doing what you ask. That is one way you express faith. Take God at His word and thank Him for His fullness. Expect that fullness to be manifested in your life.

(3) Ongoing obedience. The third key is ongoing obedience. When you, with holy desperation, make a full surrender of yourself to Christ in an act of faith and ask that the indwelling Spirit fill your life, that prayer is heard. The Spirit fills your life and begins the process of manifesting His fullness in your daily experience. The evidences may not come all at once and may not come instantly. Manifestations of the Spirit's fullness are certain—they will and do happen—but the nature and extent of the manifestations differ with each individual.

Two of God's children yield their lives to Him in entire surrender. In response to that surrender, the same event will come to both of them—a fullness of the Spirit never known, never thought possible before. But the manifestation, the experience of that fullness, will not be the same for both; . . . For God not only gives the fullness, but He also made the vessels which contain the fullness, and has made them all slightly different.[34]

Realization of the Spirit's fullness is often progressive. The act of surrender is immediate, but the revelation of strongholds of the self life, completely unrecognized before, may come gradually to your attention as the Spirit of God begins to fill and possess every corner of your being. One by one these strongholds of the fallen nature will be identified. You will be asked to open every door to every room of your spiritual house.

The question is one of walking constantly in the Spirit's fullness and power. Once the manifestation of the holy life and mighty works of Jesus have become evident, how do you remain in such a vital relationship to Christ that those manifestations will continue and increase? Every believer soon learns that being filled with the Holy Spirit is not a once-and-for-all experience. Jesus spoke to this question in His last message to His apostles on the night He was arrested (John 14:16-21; 15:4-10). Obedience to the word of God and to the leadership of the Spirit moment by moment is the simple formula for always being anointed with the Spirit's power for holy living and effective service.

As you obey God, let me make three suggestions:

First, appropriate the Spirit's fullness each day. Make practical application of Jesus' most often repeated word about the essence of discipleship: "If anyone would come after me, he must deny himself and take up his cross daily and follow me" (Luke 9:23, NIV). This means that each new day (and often crisis by crisis) the believer intentionally denies himself, takes up his cross, and chooses to follow Christ. To do this we must focus on the facts of the good news: Christ not only died for us on the cross, we also died with Him there (Rom 6:6). We count ourselves dead with Christ. We yield our bodies, minds, hearts, and wills to Him anew and afresh each day. We make him king, enthroning Him in every dimension of our lives for each new day. We surrender our mortal bodies to Him so that His life may be lived anew in our lives (2 Cor. 4:10-11).

Second, cultivate the habit of listening for God's voice and responding positively to His direction. Daily come to Him for instruction. Spend a few minutes each morning in His written Word. Listen as well as speak in a time of prayer. Always read the Word and pray with pencil and pad in hand to write down insights and instructions you may receive. Be sensitive to the still, small voice of the Spirit as He directs you daily. In doing this, learn to say yes at once. Don't delay, debate, consider, or in any other way procrastinate when He clearly speaks.

Finally, master the art of immediate confession of sin and instant appropriation of forgiveness and peace. This is what Bill Bright has called "spiritual breathing."[35] His designation is well chosen. Spiritual breathing is as essential to the Spirit-filled life as physical breathing is to physical life. To be Spirit-filled is not equal to sinless perfection. Keeping short accounts of our sins is essential to remaining Spirit-filled. "My dear children, I write this to you so that you will not sin. But if anybody does sin, we have one who speaks to the Father in our defense—Jesus Christ, the Righteous One" (1 John 2:1, NIV). We stay in step with God's Spirit; we walk and work in the power of God's Spirit, immediately turning to Christ in confession when we sin. As we agree with Him about those things we do that are wrong, His forgiving love keeps flowing into our lives.

The most important task in this life is finding others and telling them the good news of Jesus Christ. For those who say "Yes," help them to grow and become witnesses of Jesus Christ. It is our responsibility to follow Christ in obedience and faith. It is His responsibility to make us successful fishers of men. God asks only that we make ourselves available to Him, that we trust Him, and obey Him. He wants us to live holy lives and tell others about Christ in the power of His Spirit. He does the rest. The power of the Holy Spirit is available to all who will, in simple faith, make a full surrender to Him. The Holy Spirit then "works in and through the believer, producing fruit and changing the lives of those who respond favorably to his witness."[36] That responsibility belongs to the Spirit as He carries out the divine program of the Son for world evangelization.

The Program of the Son

Jesus promised the abiding presence and the awesome power of the Holy Spirit to believers. He designed a program with global dimensions for them to accomplish (Acts 1:8). Luke reported that fifty days earlier Jesus had said to them:

> This is what is written: The Christ will suffer and rise from the dead on the third day, and repentance and forgiveness of sins will be preached in his name to all nations, beginning at Jerusalem. You are witnesses of these things. I am going to send you what my Father has promised; but stay in the city until you have been clothed with power from on high (Luke 24:46-49, NIV).

This clarifies what Jesus had in mind when He said, "You will be my witnesses." He had a program of world-wide evangelism in view that would begin with the person next door. From its genesis, the mission of Jesus included "Judea and Samaria," the Jews and the Samaritans, living side by side, household by household, village by village. From His earliest, post resurrection words about the global task (Luke 24:47) to His last (Acts 1:8), Jesus distinguished the evangelistic task of His disciples from that which was being conducted contemporaneously by the Pharisees (Matt. 23:15). His disciples were sent to the ethnically diverse people of the world, even those most culturally despised by Jews. The Holy Spirit is the executor of this evangelistic mission; He is the expeditor of the evangelistic task; He is the effector of the evangelistic promise.

Executor of the Evangelistic Mission

The Holy Spirit is ultimately in charge of the evangelistic mission. He is the chief executive officer of the enterprise of world evangelization. The churches, through their various members, efforts, and organizations, are His agents to accomplish that goal. Students of management tell us that the chief executive of any enterprise has four basic responsibilities: to determine objectives and strategy, to create an effective organization for the task, to lead in the achievement of the objectives, and to keep the undertaking on track.[37] While it would not be profitable to impose these categories of the twentieth century on Acts, a perusal of the book will quickly reveal how important the Holy Spirit's role as the executive of the evangelistic mission really is.[38] An example of each of these functions will adequately illustrate the point.

He determines purpose, objectives and strategy.—"Higher authority" in any enterprise determines the purpose and objectives of that enterprise. Throughout the book of Acts, the Holy Spirit determines where the gospel will next go and how it shall be carried there.

Consider the experience of Paul and Barnabas in Pisidian Antioch. On the first sabbath, they spoke to the "men of Israel" and to the "Gentiles who worship God." The power of their appeal was such that on the next sabbath "almost the whole city gathered to hear the word of the Lord" (Acts 13:44). When the Jews rejected their message and spoke abusively against it, the response of the evangelists was to go to the Gentiles (vv. 46-47). They had appealed to higher authority for the directions and goals of their mission. They had turned to the word spoken through the prophet Isaiah by the Holy Spirit.

Consider also Acts 15. The chief issue in the Jerusalem conference was not actually whether Gentiles could be saved, though that is what the zealots from Jerusalem questioned (Acts 15:1). That issue had already been decided by the "apostles and brothers" in reference to the conversion of the household of Cornelius (Acts 11:1-18). The issue at stake was "Can a Gentile be saved without adopting the ceremonial and cultural requirements of Judaism?"

Some of the Pharisees who had become believers insisted, indeed, that the Gentiles must be circumcised and required to keep the law of Moses. Peter reminded the apostles and elders that years earlier, God had dramatically saved a group of uncircumcised Gentiles, proving it by giving them the gift of the Spirit (Acts 15:7-11). Then James arose and supported Peter (vv. 14-21). At every point in Acts, when an issue of purpose, objectives, or strategy was in question, it was the Spirit who was the ultimate authority.

He creates an effective organization.—Executive leadership is never more obvious than in the choice and deployment of personnel in an enterprise. The classic illustrations of the Holy Spirit's role in this regard can be found in Acts 8 in the surprising redeployment of Philip from Samaria to Gaza; in Acts 10 in the direction of Peter to Cornelius; and in Acts 13 in the inauguration of the Gentile mission with Barnabas and Paul.

> All believers are called to be filled with the Spirit, to demonstrate the fruit of the Spirit, and to be witnesses. Some are especially appointed and anointed as evangelists... . Through the Holy Spirit, (the risen Christ) sets apart some for special missionary and evangelistic tasks.[39]

Acts 13 reveals an additional element in organization. The Holy Spirit set the objectives and goals of the evangelistic enterprise as it was assumed by the Christians in Syrian Antioch. At the same time that the Spirit selected and called evangelists, He caused them to be recognized, set apart, sent out, and supported by the churches (Acts 13:1-3). Further, the Spirit led in creating a new structure; the evangelistic team or missionary band. Barnabas and Saul were called to divorce themselves from the nurturing of new believers and the equipping of the saints in

Antioch (Acts 11:25-26). They were commissioned to make disciples and plant churches among the dispersed Jewish populations and the various ethnic minorities that made up the Roman empire. These examples in Acts give credence to the work of the Holy Spirit in creating and manning the organizations necessary to achieve the grand goal of world evangelization.

He gives leadership to the task.—In Acts, the leadership of the Holy Spirit in the evangelistic enterprise, both directly and indirectly, is omnipresent. An illustration of massive indirect leadership by the Spirit can be found in the persecution of believers that followed the death of Stephen. Persecution caused the dispersion of Christians. Their faithfulness, under the tutelage of the Spirit, caused them to witness for Christ wherever they went. Philip fled to a city in Samaria, where he proclaimed Christ. Philip's experience in that region was only one example of what happened many times (Acts 8:1-5). Because so many were forced to flee, Peter and John were able to preach the gospel in many Samaritan villages as they were returning from their official visit there (Acts 8:25).

Some of these same people dispersed by the persecution finally arrived at Antioch and were used by the Spirit, not only to raise up believers among the Jews, but also among other ethnic groups. These men and women cannot be identified as vocational evangelists or commissioned missionaries. They were laypersons, mobile by duress, but able to share their faith spontaneously wherever they were compelled to flee.

Over and over again, throughout Christian history, laypersons, compelled by the Spirit, have borne witness to Christ in the marketplace or within the network of their extended families, neighbors, and close associates. Long before the officials of the church arrived, they were evangelistically effective and had been used by the Spirit to build up or raise up a church.

Paul's going to Macedonia (Acts 16:9-10) is an example of the direct leadership of the Spirit in the evangelistic task of the early church. The Holy Spirit intervened repeatedly and directly in the achievement of the evangelistic enterprise.

He keeps the effort on track.—The reticence of many Jewish believers to take the gospel of Christ to the Gentiles is obvious throughout Acts. The events that led to the Jerusalem conference (Acts 15), and the care taken not to offend the Jewish populace when Paul returned to Jerusalem with the offering of the Gentile believers (Acts 21:17-26) are illustrative of this hesitancy.

Had not the Spirit of God dramatically and unmistakenly manifested Himself in the conversion of the first Samaritans (Acts 8:4-17) and the first Gentiles (Acts 10:1-48), the enterprise of world evangelization may have been stalled and the intention of Jesus never realized.

Expeditor of the Evangelistic Task

All evangelism should be done with the confident realization that the primary task of giving testimony to Jesus Christ belongs to the Holy Spirit. Further, when a disciple is led by the Spirit in a witnessing situation, the Spirit Himself precedes the disciple, doing His advance work, bearing witness to Jesus Christ. He prepares, even paves the way, for the disciple's witness. The Spirit makes the words and actions of the disciples, though insignificant in themselves, powerful and effective.

He leads to receptive peoples and to seeking souls.—Steeped in individualism, Americans have difficulty recognizing social structures that are commonly perceived in nonwestern cultures: extended families, clans, tribes, casts, and even whole villages that compose a distinct cultural unit.[40] In the New Testament, multi-individual conversions were common. Whole households—which according to Acts 10:24 consisted of relatives and close friends—and entire villages turned as groups to Christ (Acts 9:35).[41] Jesus Himself saw the village of Sychar beyond the woman at the well as a field white to harvest (John 4:34-42).

This pattern in evangelism continues in many places around the world. Even in western societies, all members of nuclear families often become Christians at the same time. Churches usually grow along networks of extended families. The Holy Spirit uses these social structures in achieving His mission. Enabling personal witnesses and other evangelists to find and penetrate people groups is a work of the Spirit.

At the same time, in the New Testament, the Holy Spirit clearly led evangelists to individuals with spiritual hunger or to individuals already actively seeking God. The classic example is the mission of Philip on the road to Gaza. The encounter with Lydia at a place of prayer and the encounter with a jailor who was already spiritually prepared to ask "What must I do to be saved?" are additional examples of the Holy Spirit expediting the evangelistic task.

He opens doors of opportunity.—The Holy Spirit opens doors of opportunity for witnesses of Jesus Christ. Paul's productive evangelistic ministry in Ephesus illustrates this. The Spirit not only leads the witness to people, He also creates opportunities in cities and other geographical communities. When Paul wrote to the believers in Corinth, he explained the situation: "I shall remain in Ephesus until Pentecost; for a wide door for effective service has opened to me, and there are many adversaries" (1 Cor. 16:8-9, NASB).

Paul was eventually forced out of Ephesus amid great disappointment, heartache, and violence. However, he did not leave before the gospel had been sent from Ephesus to all of Roman Asia. Ephesus was the launching pad for sending the evangelistic message throughout this large province (Acts 19:10, Col. 1:7-8, 4:12-14). The Holy Spirit opened the doors of opportunity then and will continue to do so.

He provides words to say.—Jesus promised that when His disciples were arrested and brought before civil authorities, they would be given words to say by the Holy Spirit (Matt. 10:17-21). Just how this worked out in the early church can be illustrated by the experience of Paul. When he stood before a hostile Jewish crowd in Jerusalem, he shared his testimony as long as the mob would listen (Acts 22:1-21). The next day before the Sanhedrin, his response was entirely different. In fact, he was given words to say that actually led the Roman commander to deliver Paul from the violence of the Jews (Acts 23:1-10).

The following night, the Lord spoke to Paul, "Take courage! As you have testified about me in Jerusalem, so you must also testify in Rome" (Acts 23:11). Before Felix, he spoke about "faith in Christ Jesus" (Acts 24:10-26); before Festus, he appealed to Rome (Acts 25:1-12); and before Agrippa, he presented the claims of the gospel, pressing for a decision (Acts 26:1-29). On every occasion, Paul was given the response he needed for that situation.

This is not to suggest that the witness should neglect to prepare his presentation of the gospel or that the evangelist should refuse to develop his message to achieve the greatest impact. It does intimate that in situations of stress, during unexpected opportunities, and when ready answers are not at the disposal of the witness, the Holy Spirit can and does give just the words needed for the witnessing experience to come to a successful conclusion.

He orders providential events.—Walking in the fullness of the Spirit of God made life a wonderful adventure in the New Testament. The Spirit of God, at times, ordered events providentially so that they furthered the work of evangelism. Paul reported to the Christians in Philippi that even his imprisonment had "served to advance the gospel" (Phil. 1:12, NIV). News of Peter's ministry in Lydda and Sharon came to Joppa providentially, just at the death of Dorcas. The result of the subsequent events was that "many people believed in the Lord" (Acts 9:32-42). Paul providentially was washed up on the shores of Malta at the time when the father of Publius, the governor, was near death. The healing of the older man opened up a ministry to the whole island (Acts 28:7-10).

In these ways and others, the Holy Spirit acted to expedite the work of evangelism. Today, also, those who are led by the Spirit and are available to Him in evangelistic endeavors find life to be an exciting adventure. They are repeatedly brought into contact with people already prepared by the testimony of the Spirit to receive the message of the gospel.

As the message of the gospel is received, the Spirit performs another essential function in bringing the program of the Son to ultimate fulfillment.

Effector of the Evangelistic Promise

Finally, the Holy Spirit does the work ultimately essential to evangelism. The role of the witness in evangelism is irreplaceable, but those things ultimately essential in evangelism can be done only by the Spirit of God. The gospel promises forgiveness of sins and a new, eternal life within. The Holy Spirit brings these promises into effect.

The Holy Spirit convicts of sin.—Evangelists, by their own efforts, are unable to effect genuine conviction of sin, without which there is no turning to Christ. This essential work is done only by the Holy Spirit. Since Christ bestows forgiveness of sin, the witness may not bypass the subject of sin. To do so perverts the biblical concept of evangelism and offers cheap grace. How will people be awakened from their lethargy, confess their sin, and call on Christ to save them? They will be awakened when the Spirit comes (John 16:8-11). The Spirit convicts persons to see the gravity of sin, the possibility of righteousness, and the certainty of judgment. "Only when men are brought to acknowledge their sin is it possible for them through faith in Christ to receive righteousness and escape judgment."[42] The Spirit uses the law of God as the instrument to convict people of sin (Rom. 7:7, Gal. 3:24; 1 John 3:4). Only when the law condemns us do we look to Christ to justify us,[43] but the Holy Spirit, and He alone, is able to produce conviction of sin in our minds and hearts.

The Holy Spirit bears witness to Christ.—Conviction and witness both take place in the unbelieving world. When the Spirit comes, Jesus promised, "he will testify about me. And you also must testify" (John 15:26-27, NIV). In both personal and public evangelism, we often reverse the order. We share our witness and pray that the Holy Spirit will confirm it. Rather, we should see the Holy Spirit as the Chief Witness and our role as collaborators, using our own experience alongside of His testimony.

The testimony of the Holy Spirit is given in two forms. First, the great objective witness of the Holy Spirit to Christ is the written Word of God. The Spirit is the Author of that Word through human instruments. Our testimony confirms that written Testimony to Christ. No experience, regardless of how vivid, and no insight, regardless of how transforming, should be part of our message, if it is contrary to His testimony in the written Word.

Next, the Holy Spirit also bears an inner, subjective witness to Christ. He makes Christ known to new believers. Jesus told Peter after his great confession, "this was not revealed to you by man, but by my Father in heaven" (Matt. 16:17, NIV). Today such revelation is the Spirit's work. Just as the Son came to make the Father known, the Spirit was sent to make the Son known. This inner revelation of Christ is uniquely the work of the Spirit and is essential to evangelism. Efforts to evangelize are in vain if the Spirit of God does not do this work. Christ must be made known to the inner person or evangelistic efforts will only produce counterfeit disciples.

The Holy Spirit is the Agent of regeneration and conversion.—These two terms describe the most essential events involved in becoming a disciple. Sometimes mistakenly used interchangeably, the terms are closely related, but should be distinguished. Regeneration is uniquely the work of the Holy Spirit. The sinner, dead in sin, is made alive by the Holy Spirit. He has a new birth. Only the Holy Spirit can so re-create human beings. Jesus said, "unless one is born again, he cannot see the kingdom of God" (John 3:3, NASB). Paul said, "Therefore, if anyone is in Christ, he is a new creation; the old has gone, the new has come." (2 Cor. 5:17, NIV).

Conversion, on the other hand, is the positive response of a person to the gospel. It is humanity's responsibility. To "be converted" is to turn from sin to Christ. Conversion is the compound of those two things essential to salvation: repentance and faith. In repentance, the sinner turns from his sin; in faith, the sinner turns to God.[44] The Bible reports that people, as individuals and in groups, "turned to the Lord" (Acts 9:35, 11:21, NIV). The Bible says that evangelists actually are, in some manner, instruments of conversion. Both John the Baptist and Paul were sent to turn back to God (Luke 1:16-17; Acts 26:18).

To think, however, that conversion is something that persons can do by themselves is a mistake. People will not turn to God nor will preachers convince them to turn to God except by the work of the Holy Spirit. In the New Testament, repentance and faith are the duty of persons (Acts 2:38; 16:31; 17:30) and the gift of God (Acts 11:18; Eph. 2:8; Phil. 1:29). Ultimately, therefore, we must affirm that conversion is also a work of the Holy Spirit.

Though regeneration and conversion are inseparable, they take place according to different tables. Conversion is more of a process than an event.[45] Regeneration is instantaneous, totally a work of God. A period of time elapses during which the Holy Spirit does the work of conviction of sin and testifying to Christ. The actual time between the awakening of spiritual interest and the commitment of faith will vary.

The necessity of regeneration and conversion, and their central place in the ministry of the Spirit, constantly reminds us that those to whom the gospel is delivered are "dead" and "perishing." Good news is brought to them in order that they may be saved. Without Christ their destiny is eternal death. The good news is that in Christ, and Him alone, they have eternal life. We must be clear and dogmatic: hell is an awful, eternal reality.[46] We must be compassionate and persuasive as we tell people how to avoid hell, by turning in repentance and faith from their own way to Jesus Christ. Then all of us can say: "He saved us, not because of righteous things we had done, but because of his mercy. He saved us through the washing of rebirth and renewal by the Holy Spirit" (Titus 3:5).

Conclusion

The role of the Holy Spirit in evangelism is massive. Evangelism is His primary work. His work in evangelism is irreplaceable. Great financial resources, intellectual perception, and the creativity of human genius are not substitutes for the role of the

Spirit in evangelism. This active work of the Spirit is essential if we are to be effective in evangelism. Therefore, we should implore Him to do His work through us, to anoint and empower us, to be both faithful and effective in our evangelistic efforts.

Notes

1. "Statement Issued at the Consultation on the Work of the Holy Spirit and Evangelization," *World Evangelization* (September, 1985), 3.

2. All biblical quotations are from the New International Version except where indicated.

3. James D. G. Dunn, *Baptism in the Holy Spirit* (Philadelphia: The Westminister Press, 1970), 44.

4. Harry R. Boer, *Pentecost and Missions* (Grand Rapids: Wm. B. Eerdmans Publishing Company, 1961), 99.

5. Jean Danielou, *The Lord of History* (Cleveland and New York: Meridian Books, The World Publishing Company, 1968), 11-12.

6. John R. W. Stott, *The Baptism and Fullness of the Holy Spirit* (Downers Grove, IL: InterVarsity Press, 1964), 13.

7. The Greek preposition *en* is used only with the locative case in the New Testament. Prepositions came into being to strengthen the force of the Greek cases. The locative case is the simplest of all cases in that, wherever it is found, it indicates something located in the limits of some context. In English we represent the locative by the use of *in, on, at, among, by* (when it means a location, as by the side of), *upon,* and *beside.* See A. T. Robertson and W. Hersey Davis, *A New Short Grammar of the Greek Testament* (New York and London: Harper & Brothers Publishers, 1931), 208-273, for a full discussion of case and pronouns in biblical Greek. In the various reports of John's testimony concerning Jesus and the baptism in the Spirit, this is very important information. In Matthew 3:1 and John 1:33 the preposition *en* is used to show that baptism is *in* water and *in* Holy Spirit. In Luke 3:16 and Acts 1:5, *en* is used in reference to baptism in the Spirit but only the locative case is used to show that baptism was *in* water. In Mark 1:8, *en* is not used with either baptism in water or Holy Spirit. The locative case, however, makes it clear that the baptism was to take place within the domain of water and within the domain of Holy Spirit. The same construction is used in 1 Corinthians 12:13, baptism is *en* "one Spirit." Since the Greek word "to baptize" is correctly translated "to dip" or "to submerge," the only proper translation can be "in water" and "in the Holy Spirit."

8. Stott, *Baptism and Fullness,* 12.

9. The Spirit of the Lord came upon the seventy elders (Num. 11:25); upon Balaam, the errant prophet (Num. 24:2); upon Othniel, Gideon, and Samson, all judges (Judg. 3:10; 6:34; 14:6); and upon Saul, David, and group of Saul's men (1 Sam. 10:10; 16:13; 19:20).

10. David M. Howard, *By the Power of the Spirit* (Downers Grove, IL: InterVarsity Press, 1973), 36.

11. R. Newton Flew, *Jesus and His Church* (London: The Epworth Press, 1938), 101.

12. Boer, *Pentecost and Missions,* 113.

13. Ibid., 217.

14. Ibid., 213.

15. Ibid., 119-120.

16. J.B. Lawrence, *The Holy Spirit in Evangelism* (Grand Rapids: Zondervan Publishing House, 1954), 7.

17. G. Campbell Morgan, *The Birth of the Church*, ed. Jill Morgan (Old Tappan, NJ: Fleming H. Revell Company, 1986), 16-22.

18. Bill Bright, *Revolution Now!* (Arrow Head Springs, CA: Campus Crusade for Christ, 1969), 65-66.

19. R. A. Torrey, *The Holy Spirit: Who He Is and What He Does* (New York: Fleming H. Revell Company, 1927), 117-118. Please note that Torrey uses the terminology "baptism with the Holy Spirit" in this book, but by this term he means what I have defined as being "filled with the Spirit." For Torrey these two terms referred to the same experience. See p. 107.

20. Ibid., 119. Is Torrey right? Bezaleel, the master artist and craftsman in building the tabernacle, was filled with the Spirit for that purpose (Ex. 35:30-31). The tabernacle in the wilderness is one of the clearest pictures of Christ and His work. It would have been foolish to expect anyone not filled with the Spirit to supervise the construction of the portable temple that pointed so clearly to God's promised Messiah. Four individuals in the Gospels were said to be filled with the Holy Spirit. Three of these, Elizabeth (Luke 1:41-42), Zacharias (Luke 1:67), and John the Baptist (Luke 1:13-16), all gave powerful testimonies to the Christ when they were filled with the Spirit. The fourth person filled with the Spirit was Jesus Himself (Luke 4:1, 18), who performed His ministry, not in the power of authority of the second person of the Godhead, but as a true man, in fullness and power of the Holy Spirit.

In Acts, the evidence of people being filled with the Spirit is overwhelming. The result of the entire church being filled with the Spirit was dramatic. Many received the word of God, were baptized in water and the Spirit, and 3,000 were added to the church. Daily new believers were added to their number (Acts 2:4,41-47). Filled with the Holy Spirit, Peter bore witness to Christ in the face of imprisonment, insisting that the disciples would keep speaking what they had seen and heard (Acts 4:8,20). A little later, probably gathered with fellow believers in one of their house churches, the entire group was filled with the Spirit and spoke the word of God in boldness (Acts 4:29-31). Stephen, the witness even to death, was a man full of faith and the Holy Spirit (Acts 6:5-8). Saul of Tarsus, the new convert, was filled with the Spirit and began immediately to testify that Jesus is the Christ (Acts 9:17-20). His long, effective ministry of making disciples and planting churches was accomplished in the Holy Spirit's fullness (Acts 13:9-12). Barnabas was a man full of the Holy Spirit and, because of his life and witness, many were added to the Lord (Acts 11:24).

21. Billy Graham, *The Holy Spirit* (Waco, TX: Word Books Publishers, 1978), 104-106.

22. James H. McConkey, *The Three-Fold Secret of the Holy Spirit* (Chicago: Moody Press, n.d.), 9-42.

23. Stott, *Baptism and Fullness*, 18.

24. I am endebted to Andrew Murray for his 1895 lecture at Moody Bible Institute on this subject, though I would not totally agree with him or use the same terminology. See Murray, *The Spiritual Life* (Philadelphia: George W. Jacobs & Company, 1897), 73-88.

25. See Watchman Nee, *Love Not the World* (Fort Washington, PA: Christian Literature Crusade, 1969), 10-11 for a good introduction to the biblical uses of *kosmos*.

26. Ibid., 37.

27. Murray, *The Spiritual Life*, 116-128, and Ruth Paxson, *Rivers of Living Water* (Chicago: Moody Press, n.d.), 73-84.

28. Paxson, *Living Water*, 76. See also 77-78.

29. See James Montgomery Boice, *The Gospel of John*, IV (Grand Rapids: Zondervan Publishing House, 1978), 138-139 for a brief discussion of the various interpretations.

30. Ray C. Stedman, *Secrets of the Spirit* (Old Tappan, NJ: Fleming H. Revell, 1975), 57. I have followed Stedman in this whole paragraph.

31. McConkey, *Three-Fold Secret*, 45.

32. Bill Bright, *The Holy Spirit: The Key to Supernatural Living* (San Bernardino, CA: Campus Crusade for Christ International, 1980), 57-70.

33. Charles L. Chaney, *The Secret of the Spirit-Filled Life* (Wheaton, IL: Tyndale House Publishers, 1976), 83-87.

34. McConkey, *Three-Fold Secret*, 74.

35. Bright, *The Holy Spirit*, 57-70.

36. Bright, *The Holy Spirit*, 197. I have followed Bright in this entire paragraph; see especially 196-198.

37. Peter F. Drucker, *The Effective Executive* (New York: Harper & Row Publishers, Harper Colophon Books, 1985).

38. Alan R. Tippett, "The Holy Spirit and Responsive Relations," in *Crucial Issues in Missions Tommorrow*, ed. Donald A. McGavran (Chicago: Moody Press, 1972), 77-101. This is extremely valuable not only for its perceptive theological insights but also for its sociological perspective.

39. Leighton Ford, "The 'Finger of God' in Evangelism," *World Evangelization* (May 1986): 5-8. This is especially valuable for its fresh, sparkling interpretation of the Scripture.

40. Tippett, "Spirit and Responsive Peoples," 85.

41. Ibid., 81.

42. John R. W. Stott, *Our Guilty Silence* (Downers Grove, IL: InterVarsity Press, 1967), 93.

43. Ibid., 94.

44. John R. W. Scott, "The Biblical Basis of Evangelism," *Let the Earth Hear His Voice*, ed. J. D. Douglas (Minneapolis: World Wide Publishers, 1975), 76.

45. John R. W. Stott, *Christian Mission in the Modern World* (Downers Grove, IL: InterVarsity Press, 1975), 115.

46. Stott, "Biblical Basis," 76.

7 | The Message of Evangelism
Robert G. Hamblin

The heralding of Jesus of Nazareth and His gospel of good news has shaken the entire world for centuries. It is an explosive, life-changing, society-shaking, world-transforming message that became known as *"tu euaggelion*—the good news."[1] The gospel is the good news, but the gospel, in a word, is Jesus. Apparently the early church formed this concept in the beginning of its existence. In fact, the oldest creed of the church is, "Jesus is Lord" (1 Cor. 12:3, NIV).[2] It represents one of the most basic theological convictions early believers embraced.

The gospel is about their Lord Jesus' story. The gospel has such clearly defined content in the apostle Paul's writing that, much of the time, the "gospel" stands by itself without qualification. Furthermore, in the Gospel of Mark, the "gospel" is equated with Jesus.[3] Indeed, when the noun "evangelism" is used, it is referring to the person of Jesus Christ. "Evangelism" became flesh and brought news of the eternal Father who loved His people enough to redeem them.

Evangelism is found at the center of Christian truth. It declares through word, deed, and spirit the good news reflected in the person of Jesus Christ. It is the good news about God in Christ. Nowhere else in religious literature is the story told of a god who cares so deeply for his creatures as in the Bible. The good news has been placed in the Bible and has been given, by the eternal God, to the church as a commission to proclaim. Far more than verbal or human proclamation is implied. God participates in the redemptive action of evangelism by reaching out in personal revelation.

God has given us the job of telling a lost world of His redemptive power. Never is a person in greater need of the Holy Spirit than when witnessing for Jesus Christ. At that moment the Holy Spirit is most ready to empower a person. Evangelism, when done in the power of the Holy Spirit, persuades the unbeliever to believe in Christ, because the reality of God's love shines through.

Old Testament Backgrounds

Evangelism began with the earliest human beings. From the very beginning of the Bible, God is pictured as reaching down to us humans in order to redeem us. The themes of Genesis stand out clearly. God is the Creator. Throughout Genesis, God is revealed as seeking and caring for His people. Many have called Genesis 3:15 the pre-gospel. When God pronounced judgment upon Adam because of his sin, He tempered that judgment with a promise. God promised the offspring of woman would bring a fatal blow to the cause of sin, the serpent tempter. Many believe this is the first promise of a coming Redeemer. It is also highly reflective of people's helplessness in the face of sin and temptation. Humans needed a Redeemer.

Other passages in the Old Testament are important to an understanding of New Testament evangelism. God made a covenant with Abraham giving an entire nation hope of salvation. God's selection of the Jews was crucial to His purpose to bless the nations. They were a chosen people, a holy nation. God gave them a blessing, but also chose them to be a blessing. Where Israel failed, the new Israel is destined to succeed.

Evangelism in the Teachings of Jesus

Jesus brought into sharp focus the missionary purpose of God, which had been constantly reaffirmed throughout the Old Testament era (Gal. 4:4-5). While on earth, Jesus was chiefly concerned with teaching His followers that He was the Messiah. Such an identity was important to Jesus. After the resurrection, several themes began to emerge: the authority for evangelism (Matt. 28:18);the purpose of evangelism (to make disciples; Matt. 28:19); the method of evangelism (witnessing; Acts 1:8, Luke 24:48); the message of evangelism (the redemptive work of God and the conditions for receiving forgiveness; Luke 24:46-47); the power of evangelism (the Holy Spirit; Acts 1:8); the geography and dimensions of evangelism (neighborhoods, surrounding provinces and the uttermost parts of the earth; Acts 1:8); and the duration of evangelism (until the end of the ages; Matt. 28:20). Evangelism can be defined as the person-to-person outreach of believers to unbelievers with the gospel of Christ. It is an attempt to lead unbelievers to repentance and to personal commitment by faith in Jesus as Savior and Lord.

Evangelism is composed of several parts. These include witness, persuasion, and proclamation in varying degrees. In Acts the believers used all of the facilities God gave them as tools for evangelism. The New Testament speaks of at least two God-given motivations for evangelizing: the love of Christ and the indwelling presence of the Holy Spirit. Paul, the apostle, declared that he was constrained to evangelistic service by the love of Christ. From his statement one gets the image of a person possessed. This is how it should be. Believers should be possessed by a desire to tell. The presence of the Holy Spirit motivates people to witness and to proclaim Christ.

Key Bible Words for Evangelism

Euaggelion

The word translated "evangelism" is built upon the verb form of this Greek word. *Euaggelion* means "good news," or "gospel," in the New Testament. A study of the New Testament shows that the word it describes is clearly the act of communicating what God has done in Christ to redeem mankind.

The language of good news magnifies two theological insights. In Mark 1:1 the gospel refers to the Christ event itself. In the apostle Paul's writings, the gospel takes on the description of the crucifixion and the resurrection (1 Cor. 15). For Luke, "glad tidings" is the story of the incarnation (Luke 2:10-11). Therefore, evangelism refers to the act of announcing the good news of Christ and to the nature of the message.

The verb form for evangelism is used 51 times in the New Testament. Often both proclamation and demonstration are linked to the verb form. The noun form is used 76 times in the New Testament. The noun form is linked to the following concepts:

1. Evangelism proclaims the gospel of the kingdom, which is the authority and rule of Christ (Matt. 4:23, 9:35, 24:14).
2. It is a gospel of God. It is about God and from God (Mark 14-15).
3. It is a gospel of Jesus Christ (Mark 1:1; 2 Cor. 4:4).
4. It is a gospel which must be personally received (2 Cor. 4:3; 1 Thess. 1:5).
5. It is a gospel for all people (Mark 13:10; Acts 15:7).

Jesus is the total embodiment of what our evangelism is all about. We are not saved because we know *about* Jesus. We are saved because we have come to know *Him*, having personally experienced His presence and become acquainted with His person. We trust the living Lord as we attach ourselves to His person. "Faith, in order to be saving faith, must love beyond mental assent to trust in the person whom we call the Lord Jesus Christ."[4] Our faith becomes active as we personally involve ourselves in Christ's presence.

The good news is as relevant for the modern world as it was for the ancient world. The message of evangelism must be repeated from generation to generation, for each new generation is under the curse of sin. The gospel is the story of Jesus' personal power over death and hell. What makes that announcement so compelling is that the initiative has never been, nor will it ever be, our own. "The gospel does not originate as a human deduction, the valiant groping of humanity after a higher life; rather it comes as a message sent from heaven, the revelation of God's quest for His people, ever seeking to save the lost. To persons perishing with no sense of direction or certainty, that is good news indeed."[5]

Maturion

To this gospel we have become witnesses *(maturion)*. This word has been transliterated into English as "martyr." A long line of witnesses or martyrs have declared the reality of the gospel by their spoken word and their shed blood. New Christians can share through faith what the apostles knew firsthand. The power of their witness lay not in *their* impressions of Jesus nor *their* estimation of His person or His work. Their proclamation was *God's* mighty word spoken in light of Jesus' resurrection from the dead. His resurrection bestowed on Him power and control over all the creation for all times.[6]

The apostles spoke, told, wrote, and preached about Jesus

because they were directly illuminated or instructed. It is easy to understand why they could declare, "For we cannot but speak the things which we have seen and heard" (Acts 4:20, KJV). These early believers understood the correct meaning of the word *maturion*. They were so gripped by their encounter with Jesus the Christ that a compulsion to speak overshadowed vicious threats to their persons. They spoke as men and women who had behind them the empty tomb and before them the living Jesus.[7] Their ordinary lives were but vehicles to express the new life they found as they discovered the empty tomb and realized the impact of that first resurrection morning.

Various Words of Proclamation

The apostles were captivated with the desire to tell the good news. Accordingly, the New Testament is highlighted throughout by the rich vocabulary of proclamation language. Jesus commanded throughout every gospel and in Acts (Matt. 28:19-20; Mark 16:15; Luke 24:45-48; John 20:21; Acts 1:8) that the good news be told. In John's writings, a sister word to *euaggelion* appears. *Euaggelizō* means to proclaim, preach, or announce the good news.[8]

Paul understood that the essential nature of the gospel was to *tell* the good news. In fact, the telling of good news *(euaggelizō)* was a well-known practice in the first century, especially when it related to an important figure. The word *euaggelizō* was used in an inscription in 9 B.C. to proclaim the birthday of the Emperor Augustus. The impact of the good news about Jesus was far more significant, as the Epistle to the Romans illustrates, than the common usage of the term in the Roman Empire.[9]

Even today, the term "good news" is used to make announcements about everything. From merchandise sales to positive, newsworthy events, "good news" has come to mean anything that will bring an element of satisfaction or happiness to a world where both are at a premium. Once again contemporary Christians must impress their peers with the uniqueness of the "good news" about Jesus. It must be seen in terms of the gift of God to a world in moral, psychological, and spiritual disarray.

It was natural for Paul to think in terms of evangelizing. "In Romans 1 and 10, he clearly understood 'proclamation of the gospel' as being inherent in 'the nature of the gospel'."[10] Paul merely reflected the common desire of each Christian of that day to proclaim what they could not contain within. It is no surprise, then, that the action word *euaggelizō* appears in the Greek New

Testament so many times. The word *kērussō*, which means "to proclaim or preach," appears 61 times and is often used in tandem with *euaggelion* to describe the act of proclaiming the gospel (*kērussō-euaggelion*, Mark 16:15).

Several other words appear in the New Testament which carry the basic meaning of proclamation. *Euaggelistēs,* one who proclaims, appears three times. *Kērugma,* meaning the proclamation or the message proclaimed, appears eight times, and *kērux,* meaning preacher, appears three times. Another group of words, in addition to *euaggelizō* and *euaggelion,* are built from the stem *aggel* and appear over 80 times in the New Testament.[12]

All these words belong to a family of expressions that exhort Christians to tell the gospel. Even in this modern world of instant and mass communication, telling another person the good news, person-to-person, still remains the most effective means of gospel communication. This need for proclamation goes to the very heart of the matter. It is God's way for the recovery of sinners.

The Content of the Message

Paul and the early disciples lived in a world that was darkened by violence, cruelty, paganism, and despair. Today's world shows little change. Sensitive believers know that the need for evangelism has not ceased.[13] The challenges are the same now as they were for the early church. The world still responds to a message of goodness and hope.

The Centrality of Christ

The apostle Paul verifies the message of a Christ-centered faith. "The good news in a word, is Jesus. He is the who of the gospel, the subject and the object of our faith, and the absolutely unique fact of the Christian proclamation."[14] Evangelistic proclamation seeks to help people define their lives in terms of this unique fact. Then they can focus on the One Who has said, "I am the way and the truth and the life. No one comes to the Father except through me" (John 14:6, NIV).

Evangelism cannot be based on emotional feelings alone. It must have a strong theological base. For many reasons, evangelism must be understood theologically. Theology and evangelism are never separated in the Bible. Many doctrinal statements were made and are nourished by the evangelistic and pastoral concerns for the church. Without sound theology, evangelism degenerates into sentimentalism, emotionalism, and tactical gimmicks. Any form of evangelism that results in the manipulation of people, regardless of the motive, is unworthy of the Christ of the gospel. More tragically, this can lead to a shallow experience that falls short of genuine salvation. Scriptural evangelism demands that we fill the presentation of the gospel with solid theological content. A human soul is worthy of our best. Historically, God has honored the ministry of those who evangelize on solid theological base of the centrality of Christ.

The Nature of God

Evangelism, in terms of theology, must deal with several basic truths that are highlighted in the Bible. One of these truths is its declaration about the Almighty God. Christian proclamation begins with God. The gospel declares God is the Father who has sent His Son. This revelation is necessary to understand God's nature and to be at one with Him.

The Condition of Human Beings

Our human situation is also highlighted in the Bible. People, in their present situation, are in rebellion against God. They have sinned and come short of the glory of God (Rom. 3:23). Enough of God is revealed in nature to create guilt for the rebellion (Rom. 1:3?), but not enough is revealed to enable people to know God and receive His forgiveness in this fallen universe. Thus, it was necessary for God to reconcile humans to Himself in His Son, and to give them the ministry of reconciliation (2 Cor. 5:19).

Sin results in a broken relationship between people and God. Psychologically, alienation occurs because of sin. Sociologically, alienation from others occurs. Theologically, alienation from God occurs. Ecologically, alienation from the world occurs. Hell is the ultimate alienation because of its separation from God. This consequence of sin, coupled with the fact that all have sinned, demands evangelism.

Redemption in Christ

God has provided salvation for the human dilemma. Salvation is a result of God's action. God took the initiative. God loved the world so much that He gave His Son (John 3:16). This fact makes Christianity superior over all other religions. God has broken into human history and deals with personal needs.

Christ humiliated Himself; He became a servant who would

die for our sins (Phil. 2:5-10). His death on the cross is a deed of redemption. "This is a faithful saying, and worthy of all acceptation, that Christ Jesus came into the world to save sinners" (1 Tim. 1:15, KJV). The cross demonstrated the love of God. However, the cross was more than a demonstration. It was the provision of victory over sin (Col. 2:8-15).

Forgiveness of sins and justification for sin are provided by the redemptive deed of Jesus on the cross. What is the human response? Repentance, which means first a change of mind, then a change of the whole person. This is the first response God asks of His people. Repentance requires a turning from sin and a renunciation of sin. Faith is also a response demanded by God. Faith is a wholehearted trust in and commitment to God. It means that humans believe what God has said and done enough to act on it. Faith is the aspect of conversion in which the soul turns to Christ for salvation. As a result, Christians submit themselves to Christ as Lord.

Divine Purpose

The purpose of God is also important to a biblical understanding of the message of evangelism. God is revealed in the Bible as a sovereign God who is purposeful. He is the God of predetermination, election, initiative, promise, and fulfillment. Evangelizing the world is a part of the divine intention. He is the Savior of those who would be redeemed. Only a worldwide proclamation of the good news will provide the lost masses with the opportunity to call upon the Lord's name for salvation.

God's plan for humanity is for men and women to conform to the image of His Son. All humanity has rebelled against God. The plan of God has been distorted through disobedience. God sent His Son, the second Adam, to earth to accomplish His purpose. Jesus came in total obedience to the Father. Since then, Jesus gave a new mandate to receive the good news of salvation. It is the news of God's gracious purpose and fulfillment in Christ Jesus. It is God's purpose that the good news be carried to every person. Because its disobedience, the world deserves God's judgment; but God is offering mercy and forgiveness to all who call upon Him (Rom. 10:13).

The message of evangelism can be delivered clearly by pointing men and women, boys and girls to Jesus Christ. He is the message of evangelism incarnate. He is the good news. With the apostle Paul it can be said, "We preach Christ crucified" (1 Cor. 1:23,

KJV). That is the message proclaimed; the good news the world is entitled to hear. That is the message of salvation.

Notes

1. Michael Green, *Evangelism in the Early Church* (Grand Rapids: Wm. B. Eerdmans Publishing Co., 1970), 48.

2. Delos Miles, *Introduction to Evangelism* (Nashville: Broadman Press, 1983), 60.

3. Green, *Evangelism in the Early Church*, 54.

4. Miles, *Introduction*, 61.

5. Robert Coleman, "Theology of Evangelism," in *Review and Expositor* LXXVII (Fall 1980): 473.

6. Karl Barth, *Evangelical Theology* (Grand Rapids: Wm. B. Eerdmans Publishing Co., 1963), 29.

7. Ibid.

8. A. T. Robertson, *A Grammar of the Greek New Testament in the Light of Historical Research* (Nashville: Broadman Press, 1934), 134.

9. Kenneth West, *West's Word Studies from the Greek New Testament*, vol. I (Grand Rapids: Wm. B. Eerdmans Publishing Co., 1977), 13.

10. Francis DuBose, *God Who Sends* (Nashville: Broadman Press, 1983), 116.

11. Ibid., 117.

12. Ibid.

13. Marcus Loane, "The Evangelist's Message," in *The Word of an Evangelist* (Minneapolis, MN: World Wide Publications, 1984), 81.

14. Richard Stall Armstrong, *The Pastor-Evangelist in Worship* (Philadelphia: Westminster Press, 1986), 131.

8 | Evangelism in Our Contemporary World

C. B. Hogue

God's mandate to humanity is to know Him. He made it possible by the life, death, and resurrection of His Son. These events became good news! Jesus Christ declared that the good news must be proclaimed and witnessed to all persons until He comes again. The responsibility for sharing it is left to the contemporary believer. Theologian William Temple used the word *evangelism* to describe this responsibility: "To evangelize is to present Christ Jesus in the power of the Holy Spirit so that people shall come to put their trust in God through Him, to accept Him as their Savior and serve Him as their Lord in the fellowship of his Church." Evangelism's action never changes. The ways to accomplish evangelism are proclamation and witness.

History tends to repeat itself. The moral, social, and political life of humanity has its ups and downs. Movements occur as a result of events and experiences which either enhance or further deteriorate human existence and relationships. In these settings, evangelism has made a major impact. It is God's plan to play a major role in the improvement of humanity's spiritual, moral, and social life. The nation has been continually influenced by the work of evangelism. As democracy was being formed in the United States, attitudes and policies where being established due to influences of the eighteenth-century revival.

National growth galloped westward like wild horses into the untamed frontiers. Evangelism was a vital factor in the transformation of the moral and social beliefs of fledgling communities. Former President Theodore Roosevelt was impressed enough to say:

> The whole West owes an immense debt to the hard working frontier preachers, sometimes Presbyterian, generally Methodist or Baptist, who so gladly gave their lives to their labors and who struggled with such fiery zeal for the moral well-being of the communities to which they penetrated. Whenever there was a group of log cabins, thither some Methodist circuit-rider made his way or there some Baptist took up his abode . . . . They proved their truth by their endeavor. They yielded scores of martyrs, nameless and unknown men who perished at the hands of savages, or by sickness or in flood or storm.[1]

Despite the challenges, spirited pioneers overcame all obstacles to preach the gospel.

There were periods in history when religious fervor was lax. An increase of immorality resulted. Evangelism's heartbeat quickened when spiritual awakenings resurged in the 1850s and the early 1900s. Youth caught the challenge and sailed overseas becoming missionaries to the whole world. Unexpected and sudden spiritual awakenings have periodically erupted, producing fruitful and far-reaching results.

The contemporary scene could not be grasped without a knowledge of these last decades. In the 1960s the country was in a war it could not win in Southeast Asia. Pressure groups with inventive action and political clout arose to challenge the government, economic systems, and the social environment. Exhibitions of unrest accelerated in the cities. College and university campuses exploded with disagreements. Youth were affected by widespread disillusionment with the institutional church. Sexism was blatant, economic troubles plagued the world. A drug culture sapped the roots of society. Few signs of hope existed beyond the existential situation. Fadism festered into the perverse sores of sexual excesses, the occult and Satan worship. Members of society searched for meaning in life. The nation was hard pressed to cope with these huge problems. Naturally, churches and religious life were severely affected.

Theologian Robert B. Munger explains this decade which threatened the future of the nation in the 1970's.

> During the 1960's, widespread disillusionment with the institutional church and the growing secularism of society left little prospect for

a receptive hearing of the Gospel. The tragic Kent State confrontation shocked and sobered the student world. A new, more open religious climate began to appear on university and college campuses. The last issue of *Time* magazine for 1969 predicted the 1970's might be a decade of religious revival. The secular gods had fallen throughout the nation. Deliverance was beginning to be sought from the 'transcendent.' The writers of the essay must have been amazed at the speed and scope of their prediction's fulfillment.[2]

The Jesus Revolution

American youth had been initiated into the cult of the comfortable and had just passed through an age of disillusioned unrest. They plunged into the search for meaning, but came up empty. They sought a sense of purpose, but it was not a commodity to be secured. Peace, security, love, and hope were untouchable illusions. As in other critical times, God responded, upsetting the status quo.

Youth rejected empty options when they discovered meaning in Jesus Christ. Students, both in and out of the counter culture, overwhelmingly responded to the Christ. Changes were so rapid and dramatic that writers of the day were hard pressed to keep up. The Jesus Revolution, catapulted from one coast to the other.

A resurgence of evangelism motivated these people to express themselves differently from those in the normal institutional churches. They baptized each other in the ocean and other waters, expressed themselves in songs they could feel, and challenged the liturgy and activities of churches. Just as they had been aggressive about the counter-cultural activities, they were equally so in their open expression of personal witnessing. Revolutionary is a mild description of the significant impact. Evangelism had regressed for 10 years. Now, it reversed directions to call for deeper conviction and commitment to the Christian faith.

Renewal

A renewal movement spread simultaneously, but it lacked the same proportions. Staid and vigorously liturgical churches experienced spiritual eruptions. Clergy and laity were disenchanted with traditional expressions of church life. A new interest in the doctrine of the Holy Spirit sparked fires of renewal at various levels of church leadership. Mainline and liturgical denominations, such as the Episcopal and Roman Catholic churches, had to cope with charismatic groups. Their expressions of faith created a different climate, which affected both theology and liturgy. Charismatic experiences whetted the appetite of others in additional denominations that longed for renewal. Many Baptists became involved in charismatic activity, but it did not create serious divisions. Reemphasis of the ministry of the Holy Spirit created interest in the deeper life concepts. These renewal activities included a concern for evangelistic advance.

From Clergy Oriented to Lay Oriented Evangelism

The Jesus Revolution and the open interest in renewal conspired, unofficially, to reexamine biblical teachings of the New Testament church. An enthusiastic search for Bible truths was created by small group fellowships. Small groups, not to be shackled to sheltered sanctuaries, met in homes, businesses, restaurants, and elsewhere. A laity movement was vitalized by a renewal of personal faith.

New Testament evangelism emphasizes the witness of laypersons in their day to day life. The people of the early church witnessed in the traffic patterns of their lives. That generation of lay persons grappled with the responsibility of sharing their faith. They refused to leave it to the professionals. They rediscovered that the conversion of non-Christian believers depended more on their enthusiastic witness than it did on the witness of paid leaders whose time was taken by routine administrative and pastoral duties. Just as it was in the early days of Christian witness, once again, opportunities to witness were found in the full traffic pattern of life: in family, neighbor, and business relationships.

The movement away from clergy-oriented evangelism to lay-oriented evangelism has stepped outside existing church structures. Para-church groups have filled the void, because the organized church did not allow room for the movement in its organizations or church activities. This was and is a tragic development. The organized church was not flexible enough to permit lay-activated evangelism to blossom and be fruitful, thereby strengthening the growth of the church. Early Christianity gave strong evidence of being a lay movement.

Laypeople today are seeking to recapture the vitality and action of the early church. Historically, whenever God's special touch of awakening has occurred, the laity have spontaneously assumed responsibility for evangelistic ministry at home and in the world. The body of Christ will not win the lost in significant numbers without God-touched laypersons, whose ordinary lives become extra-ordinary witnesses to His reconciling love.

Focus on the Church on Mission

While the preceding movements have impacted church life, theological leaders have taken a more serious look at the mission of the church. Evangelical leaders have restudied the nature of the gospel, God's intention for the world, and the place of the church in the scheme of things. They share current research, pool informed opinion, and examine recent cultural, sociological, and economic trends. The recent science of futurism has even been commandeered by church and para-church leaders to assist in anticipating what will be needed to make the churches more effective. The conclusion of a variety of researchers is: evangelism remains the unchanging method for changing lives and societal living.

Theological focus on the primary task of the church has accelerated interest in church growth as a science. Specialists in this arena have varied definitions and interpretations of what church growth really is. Church growth rests upon biblical truths, extends from a rich heritage of church development, and responds to the nature of the community and congregational needs.

Some have tried to create a dichotomy between evangelism and church growth. No such dichotomy exists. The growth of any church or denomination is directly related to, and dependent on, evangelism. There are many methods and processes, but evangelism, in theological perspective, connects with the totality of Christianity. In its truest form it is holistic.

The mission of the church is a theology of hope and involvement. The late John Havlik often used the experience of Jesus with Zacchaeus for people who were speculating about the concept of evangelism. If Zacchaeus could be changed, there is hope for all humanity. If Zacchaeus could be made new, Havlik said, there is hope for a redeemed society. Believers envision the possibilities of the touch of the Risen Christ on a sinful nation and on an apparently hopeless society, but that vision requires involvement with all people who hurt and have need. The Good News speaks to and is involved in life-saving and life-changing goals for every person.

We have evidence to support the opinion that America experienced a spiritual turnaround in the 1970s. New attention to the good news, developed from the use of media, created a change of emphasis for many major denominations. Formerly, a heavy commitment to social action took precedent. That was replaced by a new concern for deep, spiritual vitality which shaped strategies for church growth. The results were for the first time in two decades, many old line denominations experienced a halt in the rate of membership decline and some had a slight moving upward again. This did not last, however, throughout the decade. Many new and growing large independent congregations give freedom to exercise the charismatic gifts; some have a strong emphasis on what has been called "signs and wonders."

A new initiative for an aggressive life-style of evangelistic practice is in order. However, be certain that evangelism stays within the scope of the Lord's example and teachings. Reason is implied by Charles Colson when he asks, "Have we so accommodated the Gospel of Jesus Christ to the twentieth century that what we offer is no more than a better way for men to achieve his humanitarian goals?" Pollster George Gallup, Jr., responded by saying that the churches must be concerned about producing, not just nice people, but new people. Thus the witness must be more than evangelism as usual.

A practicing, evangelistic life-style must listen to New Testament demands calling for all persons to be saved: "The Lord is . . . not willing that any should perish, but that all should come to repentance" (2 Pet. 3:9, KJV). Paul knew that all should have that new life-changing experience when he said "Christ died for our sins" (1 Cor. 15:3, KJV); "God was in Christ, reconciling the world unto himself" (2 Cor. 5:19, KJV); and "Knowing therefore the terror of the Lord, we persuade men" (2 Cor. 5:11, KJV). Seward Hiltner in *Ferment in Ministry* declared, "It is high time that we get evangelizing out of the theological basement. If we have a treasure to be shared with all men who will receive it, let us get on with it."

Life-style evangelism begins with a personal relationship to Jesus Christ. Such experience clarifies individuals' position as to who they are: a sinner in need of God; and who God is: the One who revealed Himself in His Son, the hope and all humanity. Professor E. G. Homrighausen describes it:

That (revelation) is a mandate God has visited us; has assumed full responsibility for us; has identified Himself with us so that nothing can separate us from His love; has borne our tragic lot and tragic perversity; has tasted our despair and death; has won a decisive victory over the powers of evil; has opened heavenly possibilities through the resurrection and the power of the Spirit.

That same message, which brought a holy compulsion into the lives of the early proclaimers, still commands its declaration today. A. T. Pierson wrote: Witnessing is a necessity for a truly redeemed soul. A light that does not shine, a spring that does not flow, a seed that does not grow is no more an anomaly than a life in Christ that does not witness for Christ. Such witnessing springs from the Word in the heart and the evidence of the holiness in one's life. Consistency of life and words harmonize into a life-style of sharing in the traffic pattern of the believer's life.

Contemporary evangelism of a life-style nature will continue to play a major role in the coming years. The challenge of believers to meet the opportunity before them has never been greater. First-century believers took Christ seriously and charged into their world, spreading the joyful good news everywhere. Contemporary believers must do the same.

The top priorities in the church are acknowledged by the actions of people who are more committed to "going than coming." If the church is to grow, the truly born-again people will mobilize their resources in a comprehensive witness. God calls His people and His churches to personal evangelism. Strategies are taking shape to answer this call. Evangelistic organizations are using the media to develop a movement. In an attempt to capture the imaginations of church members, para-church organizations propose innovative ways to spread the gospel. Major denominations are using church-growth specialists in an effort to develop strategies that offer answers to the problem of declining membership. At the same time evangelistic methods and strategies are being devised by church groups to meet the challenge of unsaved people.

Trends for Training

The average pastor who wishes to challenge his people to reach the unsaved is inundated. He must size up his situation, understand the biblical mandate, and challenge and equip his people. Together, pastor and people must complete the evangelistic task.

The church needs to become a dynamic organism with a world-wide imperative to witnessing comprehensively to everyone.

It is wise to concentrate on one general method of equipping and sending out the laypersons. They are open and willing to be trained, but many are handicapped by inferiority, defeat complexes, lack of knowledge, and fear. This is mainly because of lack of training and experience. Recognizing these problems, a training event has been devised as a remedy for doubtful discipleship. It has been amazingly successful. Most church leaders call them Lay Evangelism Schools or Institutes. Thousands of timid or ineffective witnesses have become skillful and faithful practitioners of a life-style evangelism because of these training experiences. Also, they are good opportunities for laypersons, who are already motivated to witness, to sharpen their witnessing skills.

Many other witnessing opportunities have been developed. Para-church groups, denominational leaders, and local church leaders have all been creative in devising many effective methods for training laypersons. These specific methods are readily available.

Continuing Witness Training

The early church manifested its strength with an amazing multiplication of believers. Ablaze for God and the good news, those followers of Christ attracted others to the light. There is no substitute for one friend telling another friend what Jesus can do. The person in the pew can relate the good news in the language of his or her craft or profession.

The trend to give training to the layperson will accelerate. A continuous witness training process is being validated in hundreds of churches with phenomenal results. This process equips a person who truly wants to witness for Christ by teaching assignment witnessing. The person spends 12 weeks intensely studying biblical principles and a model presentation of the gospel. He must have a general know-how of the witnessing experience. A trained person, who witnesses habitually, then becomes an equipper until a gradual multiplication of witnesses soon grows into a small force of believers ready to assault the world with the gospel.

Any church wanting to become serious about mobilizing its members has the means to do so. Both para-church groups and some denominational departments of evangelism have such training programs with a clear purpose and a capable equipping process. The pastor must want his church to be evangelistic. He must make evangelism the priority, and he and his church leaders must become actively involved in evangelism. A growing concern for genuine Christian vitality and a longing to be used on the part of the laity causes them to seek this kind of training.

Future Trends

A group of evangelical scholars met in Overland Park, Kansas, in 1978. The theme, "1984 and Beyond," dealt with an evangelical agenda. The participants noted that the age is characterized by increasing uncertainty about the future and by mounting personal and corporate anxieties. Each participant significantly called for a perspective that was realistic rather than naively optimistic or hopelessly pessimistic. In the speeches and personal give-and-take, a sense of urgency and a sense of trust rose to the surface.

Dr. Harry Evans, a participant, and then president of Trinity College, said in the college's publication, *Trinity Today:*

> The overwhelming consensus (of the participants in the consultation) was that the stance of the faithful, biblical Christian church will be more and more in conflict with society in regard to marriage, sexuality, family stability, lifestyle, and other values. There is white water ahead for the church.

At the same program, Dr. Leighton Ford said that some questions about the future of evangelism need immediate attention. He asked:

> Who are the unchurched of America?
> Why are some churches growing and others not?
> Do our evangelistic efforts produce disciples?
> Are the converts of the "born again" movement actually linking in fellowship with God's people?
> What changes are needed in our evangelistic strategy?
> What aspects of the gospel will speak most powerfully to Americans in the coming decade?

These questions still need to be answered for the year 2000 and beyond.

Efforts to estimate future trends in evangelism lead to many trails of research and concern, some going nowhere. A time of evaluation may be more useful than the pinpointing of trends.

The mission will take the trends as they arise, not forgetting that energies will be dissipated and loyalties fragmented if sight is lost of the purpose for which the believer and the church are left on the earth.

To see this world as the New Testament forbearers did, the believer must bring the liberating power of the good news to all areas of life: the market place, the job, school, recreation, and every other area of this complex society. The burning passion which gripped Paul when he said, "Woe is me if I do not preach the gospel" (1 Cor. 9:16, NASB), must be evident in all believers.

A vision of the future may determine what really happens as God's people communicate an all-out evangelism. Churches all over the land can be awakened, equipping people in witnessing outreach. New churches can be planted within reach of every person.

Spiritual Awakening

Those who seriously analyze the predicament from a biblical perspective are convinced there is need for a mighty movement of God's presence and power in the midst of the churches. Evidence indicates evangelicals will experience more renewal. Conditions exist for an awakening where the moral and social structures are anti-God, anti-church, and non-biblical. Church leaders longingly express passionate desire for a fresh breath of God on themselves, the churches, and God's people everywhere.

As in other moments of history, a great awakening will energize the churches with the touch of the Holy Spirit. Then ordinary persons will become extraordinary instruments of power. Purpose will be recovered and refreshed in ministry both to build up the body of Christ and to be witnesses in the world.

The contemporary need is clear; let the Lord's church grow in our time. Growth is impossible without God's blessing upon His people. The mandate is to grow evangelistic churches, ministering to the needs of persons outside the realm of Christian experience. Arnold Toynbee once said, "Civilization is a movement and not a condition; a voyage and not a harbor." Christian believers can respond to Toynbee by saying that we shall meet the challenge of the movement, and capture the direction of the voyage by sharing a vision of the present and eternal hope that Jesus Christ is able to redeem and transform individuals and their circumstances!

Believers can tell what Christ has done for them and parable His liberating love. That is evangelism for today—and tomorrow!

Notes

1. Theodore Roosevelt, *The Winning of the West,* 6 vols. (New York: Current Literature Publishing Co., 1905), 6:175.

2. *Southwestern Journal of Theology* (Spring, 1976): 41.

9 | The Laos in Evangelism
Owen Cooper

There are approximately 2 billion people in the world who have reached the age of accountability and are dead in trespasses and sins. The Scripture says, "The Lord is . . . not willing that any should perish" (2 Pet. 3:9, KJV). Jesus also said, "Whosoever will, let him take the water of life freely" (Rev. 22:17, KJV). Paul wrote, "For whosoever shall call upon the name of the Lord shall be saved. How then shall they call on him in whom they have not believed? and how shall they believe in him of whom they have not heard?" (Rom. 10:13-14, KJV).

The Problem of the Church

Approximately 600 million adults proclaim to be Christians, but most are inactive in carrying the light of truth to the darkness of error which enslaves so many. Approximately 200 million adult evangelicals are inactive, yet they know "God so loved the world, that he gave his only begotten Son, that whosoever believeth in him should not perish" (John 3:16, KJV), and "he that believeth not is condemned already" (John 3:18, KJV), but fail to cast off their shackles and exercise the power God has available for them. Millions of adult church members are seemingly bound by tradition, by custom, by misinterpretation of the Scriptures, by noncommitment, or other reasons and stand idly by while millions of unbelievers pass into eternity each year without having heard of

Jesus. Meanwhile the penetrating words of the Son of God should be ringing in the ears of everyone, "Unbind them and let them go."

What binds mature Christians causing them to be unconcerned about their biblical role as unordained Christian ministers? It immobilizes them from fulfilling the commission of going into all the world to teach, preach, and make disciples. This commission has more than a geographical implication. It also has a vertical dimension and commissions us to go into the worlds of finance, of commerce, of industry, of the professions, of agriculture, of production workers, of maintenance workers, of operators of small business enterprises, of teaching, or innumerable other vocations, and preach, teach, and make disciples. What can be done to "unloose" this source of Christian power to be a force for witness, evangelism, and service in the world?

Today's Greatest Heresy

I believe that the greatest heresy in the church today is that we have divided the people of God into two groups: The first group is comprised of pastors, teachers, missionaries, and other ordained people; they are to fulfill their call in Christian work. The second group is denominated as "laypersons"; they are considered as without a call, without a ministry, largely exempt from the Great Commission, and relegated to a second-class position among the people of God. The church has no proclaimed theology to undergird these second-class citizens nor to authenticate their priesthood resulting from being believers. I find no basis in the Scripture for this division. There seems to be no theological justification for it, and it has resulted in irreparable losses to the kingdom of God.

I looked up the words "layman" and "laity" in a dictionary. Here are the most common definitions: Layman: 1. "a person who is not a clergyman." 2. "a person who does not belong to a particular profession or who is not expert in some field." Laity: 1. "the people of a religious faith as distinguished from its clergy." 2. "the mass of the people as distinguished from those of a particular profession or those specifically skilled." The important point of these two definitions is that persons are divided into two categories—ministers or nonministers; professionals or amateurs; skilled or unskilled. Members of the *laos*, all the people of God, have been divided into separate classes. That is not scriptural.

Michael B. Poore writes:

> The early Christian church that grew up as a result of the teaching of Jesus and the Apostles was unique in several ways. One of the most notable of these features was the absence of a professional religious class.
>
> However, within one hundred years of the writing of the New Testament there had grown up a system of church government that concentrated power in the hands of an elite class—the clergy, which was under the direction of bishops.
>
> By early in the second century parallels were drawn between the Christian ministry and the priesthood of the Old Testament: the high priest (bishops), priests (elders), levites (deacons), and the laity. This scheme, which was developed by Clement of Rome, set the stage for the later development of the monarchial episcopacy. Clement held that special tasks are reserved for the bishops, elders and deacons while "the layman is bound by the ordinances concerning the laity." Thus the distinction between clergy and laity was established reserving certain special functions for the clergy and relegating the layman to a subordinate position.
>
> From this point, the gulf widened so much that by the fourth century Eusebius reported two separate callings: one for those who would be perfect and must therefore be separate from the world; one for those who remain in the world and must therefore accept an inferior state of piety.

In the Old Testament it was easy to determine who were the priests. The sons of Levi were the priests. If you were not a son of Levi you were not a priest. It is very difficult in the New Testament to draw a line of distinction between the priests or pastors, and those who are not. The New Testament does not say that one should be ordained and live under different obligations to God. God paid the same price for everyone's salvation.

At the Mount of Olives where the disciples had assembled prior to the ascension of our Lord, Jesus turned to them and addressed each personally. He said, "You, all of you, are to participate in carrying on the work after I am gone by witnessing where you live, in the adjoining areas, in neighboring countries and throughout the world" (Acts 1:8, author's translation). Earlier he had said, "As you are going into all the world, witness and teach and preach and make disciples" (Matt. 28:19, author's translation). This injunction was given to all Christians, not just the apostles, the ordained, and the missionaries.

Jesus utilized a brilliant theologian and highly trained individuals to contribute immeasurably to the spread of the gospel. When the great persecution arose in Jerusalem the people were scattered everywhere "except for the pastors" (Acts 8:1, author's translation); they stayed in Jerusalem. The members of the *laos* were scattered abroad. They went everywhere preaching the word and many were saved. Today this would be called a simultaneous evangelistic crusade. It was a group of the *laos*, not apostles, that went to Phoenicia, Cyprus, Antioch, and other places spreading the gospel (Acts 11:19). Pastors simply cannot do the job alone. They need the help of the laypeople of God.

The modern church is not receiving enough participation from most of the *laos*. Church members need to be trained for their ministry. Most church members have developed an unholy contentment, with the average member of the *laos* sitting in the pew Sunday morning, making a reasonable contribution to support the program and work of the church, contributing to special offerings, helping build a new building, attending Sunday School, and not becoming an irritant in the church. This is the great heresy. It is necessary to develop an adequate and satisfactory "theology of the ministry of the unordained." This theology would help utilize the greatest unused human resource available to the church: the noninvolved members. It is imperative that this resource be recognized, understood, and provided with an adequate theological base so that they, too, may feel comfortable in "walking worthy in the vocation wherein they were called" (Eph. 4:1, author's translation).

Those who believe in the preisthood of all believers could unleash a tremendous additional force in the world by putting into practice what they believe. By recognizing that there is a call for every believer, that every believer has a ministry, providing channels through which all believers may find fulfillment in their ministries, and developing a generally accepted, biblically based theology, the *laos* could help win the world to faith in Christ.

Dr. Richard C. Halverson, Chaplain of the U.S. Senate writes: "It takes *relatively few* of the people of God to do 'church work' —that is *keep ecclesiastical machinery going . . . . It takes all the people of God to do 'the work of the Church'*—which has to do with what they are doing *between Sundays* when they are invisible as a corporate entity—when they are *dispersed into the world*—when they disappear into the fabric of society."

The Barrier in the Church

Here are some suggestions that I would like to make to help erase a barrier between the pulpit and the pew, to help eliminate the concept of two classes of obligations and responsibilities for Christians, and to help get all the people to recognize that they are members of the *laos*, the people of God, with a corresponding commitment that should inevitably follow becoming a child a God.

At the outset we should seriously consider altering the standards for recruiting. If our standard is recruiting people to become members of a large congregation so that a large church can be built and more people become members to provide more money to build a larger building, that is the type member we will get.

If we recruit numbers we will get numbers. I know of no organization easier to join, easier to maintain membership, easier to fulfill minimum memberhsip requirements, than a church.

If we recruit more ministers we will get more ministers. If we recruit those who will visit, we will get more visitors. If we recruit with the idea that members should witness, we will get more witnesses. If we recruit with the concept that everyone is a missionary, we will get more missionaries.

The story of Gideon shakes me up. I am not wise enough to apply it to local churches. Perhaps many of you can make the application. Maybe it isn't how many but how much; not how large but how strong; not how big but how committed.

Elton Trueblood likened the clergyman to a coach of a football team. The coach instructs, teaches, motivates, and helps direct the play, but the team (the unordained) has the major role in actually playing the game. Or perhaps we can see the ordained minister as a filling station attendant. The layman gets his car filled up with fuel and kept in repair by the man at the station, but the unordained does the actual running of the car, not the attendant or the mechanic.

At the same time, the ordained leadership are Christians, too. They must also "play the game" and "drive a car." This is essential because they are Christians, not because they are ordained. In other words, one of the chief duties of the ordained leader is a helper, an equipper of the unordained so that they can get on with the task—not vice versa, as is so often the case.

I challenge any pastor to make a list of the things he should do as an ordained person then scratch off all items not required of him as a Christian;then use the residual list as a standard and challenge to be followed by the congregation.

Need I say that I believe that within our church, sitting complacently in the pews, there are many with a gnawing hunger of unsatisfaction in their hearts, there are countless thousands, yea, even millions, who need to be recruited, trained, and put on the Lord's team?

Living Up to Expectation

Each person chosen by God has been denominated as a priest or minister numbered among the saints (1 Pet. 2:29). It makes every Christian something special. All those who serve in places of leadership should let the masses of Christians know of God's expectations. People will rise to the level of expectations. Every "child of the King" will not necessarily act as a child of the King, but most will if they know, beyond a shadow of a doubt, that they are truly a child of the King. Most ambassadors will act with diligence and commitment if they know they are serving with appropriate and approved credentials from the sovereign power they represent.

Motivators claim there is something within that responds to the challenge of high expectations. The average church has a very low level of expectation from those who occupy the pew. Christ said that "unto whomsoever much is given, of him shall be much required" (Luke 12:48, KJV). Can churches have a level of expectation so low that it does not challenge the two-, five-, or ten-talent bench-warmer? And could this be the reason so many of them become heavily involved with their time, energy, mental ability, and finances with para-church and civic related activities?

There is a need to multiply many times the channels and places through which to serve God in our churches, local associations, state meetings, national and world meetings. This can be done by opening new and challenging places of service and involvement to the unordained.

Most members of boards and commissions of the major denominations are filled by ordained ministers. Less than half of the remaining places are available to challenge the millions of unordained members of the churches. Few laymen are vitally involved in associational and state activities. Only in recent years have large numbers of laity had an opportunity to become involved in home and foreign mission activities, and these have been more the initiative of the individual than the program of the mission agency. All too often, gifted laypersons have been frustrated in their desire for meaningful involvement in denominational activities and hence turned to para-church groups for an opportunity for meaningful involvement and rewarding participation. This is not as it should be. There is nothing in the Scripture to indicate that a Christian should sit idly by and await the church or a denominational organization to offer meaningful involvement. Christians are to act using their time, talents, and finances as the gospel is spread.

The Calling to Ministry

In a very interesting paper by Dr. George Peck of Andover Newton Theological School on the subject "The Call of the Ministry: Its Meaning and Scope," it is stated that in the Old Testament we have "the election of Israel, the calling of the whole community, to the acknowledgment, the worship and the service of God, all men are called to do this. To be an Israelite meant to be subject to such a call."

Dr. Peck also points out within this general call some were summoned further by God to specific roles: Moses for leadership; Joshua for the military; Gideon for a judge; Aaron as a priest; David as a King; Isaiah as a prophet. Furthermore, in the New Testament, the concept of the call is also evident. Every Christian has a call into the body of Christ, into the church, into a relationship with God through Christ. This is the same overall call as in the Old Testament, the call to membership, the call to service, then specific calls to particular responsibilities. John wrote; "Ye have not chosen me, but I have chosen you, and ordained you, that ye should go and bring forth fruit" (John 15:16, KJV). According to Dr. Peck all Christians have a call to serve Christ.

Dr. Lewis Drummond, Billy Graham Professor of Evangelism at Beeson Divinity School, commenting upon the statement of Michael Green in his book *Evangelism in the Early Church* writes,

> Ministry for the early Christians—all of them—was a happy, unconscious effort. They (all) went about quite naturally sharing their faith, serving and ministering as they were able. They were zealous, enthusiastic; they could not help but speak the things they

had experienced. They were not professionals; they were unpaid. As a consequence they were taken seriously—especially was this true in the lower classes and the movement spread like wildfire.

Dr. Drummond further comments,

> It is reasonably conclusive that in the early church there was little if any distinction between full-time, ordained ministers and the laity, at least in the sense of responsibility to spread the good news and minister in the name of Christ. Every Christian was in some sense a God-called minister. This principle rests in the fact that God's Holy Spirit imparts to all believers certain "spiritual gifts" to enable them to serve Christ effectively.

This does not mean that dedicated, well-trained, paid professionals are not necessary, including pastors, missionaries, and others. The point I am trying to make is that our present method of depending on "paid workers" to usher in the Kingdom or to win the world to Christ is not viable. The next great upsurge of Christianity awaits the involvement of the *laos*—all the people of God.

All Christians are commissioned to be witnesses according to Acts 1:8. In the first verse of the eighth chapter of Acts a great persecution against the church in Jerusalem is found. The unordained peoples scattered abroad, but the apostles, the ordained, remained in Jerusalem. In Acts 8:4 all of these unordained went everywhere witnessing—the true role of every Christian.

There is a strange, almost inexplicable, stirring among the unordained of the churches. There are manifestations of a desire and willingness for a greater involvement in helping achieve the objectives of denominational work. There are outcroppings of activities where church members are involved in programs outside their denomination because they cannot find an existing channel through which they can become meaningfully involved.

This occurrence could be the result of listening to the voices of leaders as they talk about carrying the word of witness to every person by the end of this century. There is a conscious and, at times, an unconscious response from the person in the pew expressing the desire to take part.

Perhaps it is the movement of the Holy Spirit from within, reminding laypersons of the vast resources available to individuals and to their denomination (John 4:35, Matt. 9:37). It could be Christians' ears are more sensitized and their hearts more receptive to the call of God. He has a call for all of His children and that call is not reserved exclusively for the ordained. This quickening among the unordained is an actuality. It is coupled with many questions raised in the minds of the unordained that need a theological answer.

When a scripturally based theological answer has been given to the questions and the answers synthesized, a theology will exist for the unordained. When such a theology is taught in the seminaries, proclaimed in the pulpit, and practiced by the pew, the unordained will activate. This great army of God can march forth and provide the prayer, the plan, the funds, and the manpower to witness to every person before the end of this century.

10 | Spiritual Awakenings and Evangelism
Lewis A. Drummond

Introduction

> No person seemed to wish to go home—hunger and sleep seemed
> to affect nobody—eternal things were the vast concern. Here awak-
> ening and converting work was to be found in every part of the
> multitude... sober professors, who had been communicants for
> many years, now lying prostrate on the ground, crying out in such
> language as this: "Oh! How I would have despised any person a few
> days ago, who would have acted as I am doing now! But I cannot
> help it!"... persons of every description, white and black, were to be
> found in every part of the most extreme distress.[1]

With these words James McGready gives his account of the
great frontier revival that burst out in Logan County, Kentucky,
in 1800. This significant awakening was the westward thrust of
the Second Great Awakening that had begun in 1792 in the New
England states. It traveled down the east coast on the wings of the
Spirit, and continued to make its way through the Cumberland
gap as the revived frontiersmen moved westward in the early
days of the dynamic 19th century. Revival was flaming throughout the countryside of the newly formed United States of America
and multitudes were being caught up in the conflagration.

Spiritual awakening is not a new phenomenon, however. The
Bible and church history both abound in movements considered
revival, spiritual awakening, or refreshing times from the Lord.

117

These significant times are the answer to the fervent prayer of God's people as they resonate with the psalmist's to God,

> Restore us again, O God of our salvation, and put away thy indignation toward us!
> ....
> Wilt thou not revive us again, that thy people may rejoice in thee? (85:4,6, RSV).

These profound movements raise a very significant question: As refreshing to the church as such times obviously are, do people get *genuinely converted* and is the evangelistic impact of an awakening experience truly significant? A quick survey of the Bible and church history will help to answer this question.

Spiritual Awakening in the Bible

Insight can be gained by looking at some of the monumental moments when God poured out His Spirit in an unusual manner on His people as recorded in the Scriptures.

The Old Testament

The Old Testament is filled with such incidents. Jonah, the reluctant, rebellious prophet, was dramatically arrested by God during his flight from his responsibilities. He found himself in the belly of a great fish. After his own personal revival that produced a yieldedness to God's will, he turned to the great city of Nineveh. Subsequently, God did one of His great redemptive things. The entire population prostrated themselves before the glory of the Lord. The Ninevites believed God, repented of their sins, turned from their idols, and a true spiritual awakening dawned. This is clear biblical evidence that the evangelistic impact is tremendous during a reviving time.

Young King Hezekiah had a very inauspicious beginning to his reign. He had inherited profound spiritual problems. His father and his grandfather were wicked rulers of Judah. The nation floundered in a deep moral and spiritual slump. Hezekiah began to pray, work, exercise his influence, and soon a mighty spiritual revival came to the people of Israel. Multitudes repented, turned to God, and found a living vibrant relationship with Yahweh.

This type of circumstance is repeated throughout the Old Testament. Due to those high, holy moments when God sent true revival, Israel was saved many times. It is in divine moments of time that deep and profound repentance and genuine seeking of God ensues.

The New Testament

In the New Testament, however, the principle of spiritual awakening blossoms in all of its beauty. In the Book of Acts, chapters 1 and 2 present the prototype of what a church should be. Acts 1 reveals the disciples got their priorities right by grasping the fact that their primary responsibility was witnessing. (Acts 1:8). Then, by making preparations through prayer (v. 14), and establishing the church on good foundations (vv. 15ff.), they were ready for the Pentecostal outpouring. Acts 2:1-4 gives the Pentecost event that dramatically thrust Jerusalem into turmoil. Acts 2:6,7,12 tells us the people were "amazed" and "perplexed." Finally, they threw up their hands in despair and cried out "What does this mean?" In answer, Peter stood up and preached and 3,000 were converted that day.

Moreover, the infant church, "devoted themselves to the apostles' teaching and fellowship, to the breaking of bread and the prayers" (Acts 2:42, RSV). Verse 47 holds the capstone of that great Pentecostal chapter: "the Lord added to their number day by day those who were being saved" (RSV). The tremendous Pentecostal revival brought multitudes to faith in Jesus Christ. The church's entire evangelistic ministry was launched in the setting of that great spiritual awakening.

Thus the pattern for what the church should be is established. Whenever a church falls short of these essential principles it needs to be revived so its evangelistic ministry can have an impact upon the contemporary world.

From Constantine to Calvin

For the first 300 years of Christianity, the church burned with committed zeal, and the Mediterranean world was brought to the foot of the cross. Then the tragic thousand years of the "dark ages" settled in. Even in those dismal days God granted some refreshing times. The ministry of some spiritual giants was performed. Such personalities as Bernard of Clarvioux, St. Francis of Assisi, and Savonarola, the monk of the Dominion order who ministered in Florence, Italy, in the dynamic 15th century were active during these depressing times. Even in the

Middle Ages, there were still times of real revival and effective evangelistic outreach.

On October 31, 1517, another monk, Martin Luther, nailed his 95 theses to the Wittenberg Church door and the great Reformation burst on the European continent. Through Luther, John Calvin, Ulhdrich Zwingli and others, tremendous reformation and evangelistic work was undertaken. The revival came when the biblical truth, "The just shall live by faith" (Rom. 1:17, KJV), was held high. As a consequence, multitudes pressed into the kingdom as the evangelistic message of Jesus Christ impacted the nations. However, in the lifetime of the reformers themselves deterioration once more set in. Revival comes, and revival goes. Luther said that a spiritual awakening lasts only 30 years.[2]

The Puritan-Pietistic Awakening

Puritan Leaders

God stimulated new reviving and awakening work in a theological institution, Cambridge University in England. A young professor began to impact his students profoundly. William Perkins became one of the founding fathers of a great reviving, reforming movement called the Puritan-Pietistic awakening. Puritanism and Pietism have not enjoyed a very good reputation in some circles, because of the writings of certain historians. Oftentimes their writings are quite erroneous. The Puritan-Pietistic movement proved to be a great time of spiritual renewal. The Puritans and Pietists were not the mean, legalistic killjoys as some people have viewed them. They were a happy, revived people.[3]

Soon all of Europe was caught up in the blessings of the new awakening. A beautiful chain reaction soon followed. The British Puritans touched many leaders: William Aimes, Lodenstein, and Tellink of Holland. A man from northern Germany named Theodore Untereck attended the University of Utrek in Holland. He was filled by the Puritan-Pietistic spirit and went back to Germany, spreading the new spirit of revival into the old Lutheran stream.

The Rise of Pietism

In Germany God raised up mighty men, such as John Arndt whose book, *True Christianity,* graced every Lutheran home. Others significant in the awakening were Philip Spenner, the mighty preacher of Berlin, and his protege, Herman August Francke, who became professor of Theology at the University of Halle. This Pietist educator influenced hundreds of young students; one of whom was Count Ludwig von Zinzendorf. After the Count finished his theological education, he went back to his lordly estate called Herrnhut, and began to provide refuge to persecuted Moravian brethren. In that setting, Moravian revival erupted. The outpouring of the Spirit brought the missionary-evangelism thrust into the Puritan-Pietistic awakening. The Moravians went everywhere sharing the gospel of Jesus Christ. Millions were impacted with the good news.

The Evangelical Revival in England

Meanwhile, in Britain where the movement had its beginning, a young, disturbed Anglican priest sailed to America to do work among the American Indians. He met some Moravian missionaries on the journey. A raging storm swept over the little ship. The poor priest was terrified. Yet, the Moravian missionaries were calm due to their deep abiding faith. Their serenity shook the priest tremendously. John Wesley spent three years in America, sailed back to London only to pen in his journal, "I went to America to convert the heathen, but oh, who will convert me?"[4]

In London, another Moravian—Peter Bohler—impacted John Wesley significantly. Then a short time later, a further situation is found in the young priest's journal:

> Wednesday, May 24th, 1738. In the evening I went very unwillingly to the Society in Aldersgate Street, where someone was reading Luther's preface to his epistle to the Romans. About a quarter before nine I...I felt my heart strangely warmed. I felt I did trust Christ, Christ alone for my salvation; and an assurance was given me, that He had taken away my sin, even mine, and saved me from the law of sin and death.[5]

John Wesley came to faith in Jesus Christ. Then, joined by his brother Charles and his close friend George Whitefield, they instigated the great Wesley-Whitefield revival. God so mightily awakened the British, that historians declare the 18th century awakening saved Britain from the bloody fate of Paris during the tragic time called the French Revolution.

Now the circle was complete; from Perkins to Aimes, to Lodenstein, and Untereck; through Arnt, Spenner, Francke Spenner, Zinzendorf, and the Moravians, back to Britain through

John Wesley—the great Puritan-Pietistic revival transformed all western Europe.

Revival in America

During the time of this circular development, sorties were constantly being sent to America. George Whitefield himself came to the new-world seven times. On his last trip he died on the Saturday night after preaching to a multitude in the town of Newburyport, Massachusetts. He is buried in the Old First Presbyterian Church in a little crypt.

First Great Awakening

The First Great Awakening in America came through the preaching of Whitefield and other notables, such as Jonathan Edwards, the Tennents, and Frederick Freylinghusen. Edward's famous sermon, "Sinners in the Hands of an Angry God," remains a classic of early American literature. The First Great Awakening transformed the colonies. The number of people that came to faith in Jesus Christ is uncountable. Evangelism expanded as it had never done in the early American colonies.

But again the deterioration set in. The Revolutionary War took a dramatic toll on the morals, ethics, and spiritual life of young America. J. Edwin Orr put it;

> In the wake of the American Revolution there was a moral slump. Out of a population of 5 million, 300,000 were confirmed drunkards. They were burying 15,000 of them each year. Profanity was of the most shocking kind. For the first time in the history of the American settlement, women were afraid to go out on the street at night for fear of assault. Bank robberies were a daily occurrence. What about the Churches? The Methodists were loosing more members than they were gaining. The Baptists said they had their most wintry season. Kenneth Scott Latourette, the great church historian, wrote: It seems as though Christianity was about to be ushered out of the affairs of men. The Churches had their back to the wall seeming as though they were being wiped out.[6]

The Second Great Awakening

God raised up a handful of men who called the young nation to a "Concert of Prayer" for revival. Baptist historian and preacher Isacc Backus, along with 23 others, called the country to intercession—and the people responded. In 1792 the Second Great Awakening began and God mightily revived individuals, churches, and entire communities. The western movement had also begun. This brings us to the great Logan County revival under the preaching of James McGready mentioned earlier. This movement gave birth to the camp meeting. The next summer, Barton Stone, pastor of the Cane Ridge Meeting House in Bourbon County, Kentucky, called for a similar meeting. Even though this was a small country church on the western frontier, 20,000 people arrived. The whole nation was ablaze with the gospel. The Second Great Awakening produced the dynamic ministry of Charles G. Finney, a man so powerful virtually entire communities would come to faith in Christ in a matter of weeks through his preaching-evangelistic ministry. Evangelism flourished. In Kentucky alone, from 1800 to 1803, Baptists tripled and Methodists quadrupled in church membership.

The Laymen's Prayer Revival

The Second Great Awakening had its day, and again, stagnation set in. Then, in 1858, a lay missionary of the Dutch Reformed congregation on Fulton Street in New York City, called the people to prayer during the noon hour. Jeremiah Lamphier made revival history. His first prayer meeting, however, was very inauspicious. Only six people arrived, and they were half an hour late. Nevertheless, they decided to have another prayer meeting the next week. On this occasion 16 people arrived. From there, the responses escalated. In a few months every church building, theatre, and auditorium was filled during the noon hour as people came to God in earnest prayer. The revival swept across the entire nation from New York City to Seattle, Washington. Church bells rang three times a day, calling the faithful to prayer. For the next two years, 50,000 converts a month were added to the churches. (There were only 30 million people in America.) This tremendous revival had an unbelievable evangelistic impact. The Layman's Prayer Revival of 1858 prepared the nation for the holocaust called the Civil War. Even during the war years, significant revivals occurred in the Union and Confederate armies as the impact of the Prayer Revival continued reaching people for Jesus Christ.

The Latter Rain Revival

In the little country of Wales, the Great Welsh Revival began under the preaching of 26-year-old Evan Roberts. That movement of 1904 was not just a small revival in a corner of the British Isles.

It engulfed all of Britain and spread across the Atlantic. By 1905 it reached America. One illustration will suffice to show the evangelistic impact of this revival. In 1905, Dr. J. J. Cheek, pastor of the First Baptist Church of Paducah, Kentucky (a small town and congregation in that day), dedicated himself to the winning of souls. The pastor said, "I will give myself to the salvation of souls." In the next two months, Dr. Cheek took into the fellowship of the First Baptist Church of Paducah nearly 1,000 new members and literally died of overwork. *The Western Recorder*, a Kentucky Baptist paper, eulogized him with these words: "A glorious ending to a faithful ministry."[7]

Contemporary Revivals

There are many prime opportunities in the world today. A revival has been going on in East Africa for decades. Hundreds of thousands have come to faith in Christ. The great Indonesian revival of a few years ago brought two million people to Jesus Christ. Practically all are knowledgeable of the great awakening that is coursing through Korea. Recently, I had the privilege of ministering in Seoul, Korea. I preached to a Friday night prayer meeting. People came to pray through the night. Between 15 and 20 thousand people were in attendance during this all-night prayer meeting. Thousands are being won to faith in Christ weekly. Today, in Korea, the church is growing four times the rate of the general population growth. The evangelistic impact of the Korean revival is beyond measure. One church has grown to over 500,000 members.

The history of spiritual awakenings is truly glorious. The evangelistic emphasis and impact that springs out of these refreshing times almost defy imagination. Surely, it causes us to concur with the Psalmist, "Wilt thou not revive us again, that thy people may rejoice in thee?" (Psalm 85:6, RSV).

Revival Principles

Several principles always emerge, when reflecting on what actually happens in the context of a true spiritual awakening.

The "Fullness of Time"

The first basic principle of revival states that a spiritual awakening always comes in the "fullness of time." God's providential working brings factors to bear that precipitate the "fullness of time" for revival. Such was certainly the case in 1927 in the province of Shuntung, North East China. In the providence of God several missionaries had been sent to the seaport city of Chefoo because of the political unrest inland. There, the missionaries began to pray earnestly for themselves and for the Chinese Christians they had left. A profound renewal began in the hearts of those praying servants of God. When the political situation corrected itself and they were able to return to their field, revival broke out all over Shuntung province. Soon the entire nation was aflame with the gospel of Christ. Multitudes entered the kingdom, the churches grew dramatically and the theological training institutions were flooded with new candidates for the ministry. This movement continued until the Japanese invasion of 1936. God had brought all factors together. Those divine factors finally precipitated in the "fullness of time."

Cleansing

The second principle of revival can be called "the principle of cleansing." It was Tuesday morning, February 3, 1970, in Wilmore, Kentucky. Situated in the heart of the village is Asbury College and Theological Seminary. On that particular Tuesday morning a professor was about to deliver the daily chapel message at the college. He decided to ask the students to share their spiritual experience. One young man stood and said to his fellow students, "I have been a phony. You all think I am a dedicated Christian; yet, there has been no reality of Christ in my life. But last night, I met the Lord." With those words God simply rent the heavens, and for the next five days, 24 hours a day, the chapel of the Asbury College overflowed with students. It took that long for those revived students to confess their sins and make restitution. In revival there is always a period of profound confession, cleansing of sin, and the healing of ruptured relationships. Many times the heart of that confession and restoration is the rekindling of zeal for evangelistic outreach.

Overflowing

The third principle involves the overflowing joy of the Lord. As our gracious God pours out the fullness of the Holy Spirit, He empowers His people for ministry and evangelism. Charles Finney, the revival preacher of the Second Great Awakening, was a 29-year-old lawyer when he came to Christ. He had a glorious conversion and an experience of the infilling of the Spirit's power. He put it in this way:

> I was powerfully converted on the morning of the 10th October, 1821. In the evening of the same day I received overwhelming (infillings) of the Holy Spirit, that went through me, as it seemed to me, body and soul. I immediately found myself endowed with such power from on high that a few words dropped here and there to individuals was the means of their immediate conversion.[8]

In true revival, the Holy Spirit fills His people with joy and power so their witness and Christian service might be more powerful.

Missions and Evangelism

The fourth great revival reality revolves around the principle of missions and evangelism. Earlier, reference was made to a prayer meeting in Seoul, Korea. In that congregation, pastor Paul Yongi Chou reaches and baptizes into the fellowship 10,000 new converts each month. It has become the largest church on earth. There has never been a revival without the work of a tremendous evangelistic ingathering. It is important to connect the evangelistic thrust with a spiritual awakening. This is a vital principle to grasp. A nation that does not periodically receive a mighty outpouring of the Holy Spirit soon degenerates into secularism and humanism. The moral spiritual foundations of the nation erodes until the society eventually collapses. Without revival, the churches dry up and the evangelistic fervor fades away and sterility sets in. Revival and evangelism coincide. It is the great revivals that have invariably brought great evangelism.

Social Action

The vital fifth principle of revival is social action. Social concern surfaces when God comes among His people during revival seasons. In the 18th-century awakening, John Wesley started credit unions, hospital work, prison reform, and a host of social ministries. William Wilburforce stopped the slave trade in Britain. George Whitefield instituted orphanages. Historically every great social movement has had its birth in spiritual awakening. Social action and evangelism are not in opposition. Revival meets the total needs of people.

Theology and Doctrine

Principle number six deals with theology and doctrine. When a church or denomination erodes ethically, morally, and spiritually, it also deteriorates theologically. However, when revival comes, there is a return to basic, apostolic, evangelical faith. This alone, ultimately solves theological problems. The great Reformation of the 16th century is a classic case in point.

The Rise of Leadership

The seventh revival principle, as one author expressed it, is the "emergence of the prophet."[9] God uses people primarily, not schemes or programs. What sort of prophet does God raise up for revival? First they are people full of *purpose*. John Wesley and George Whitefield set their faces like a flint to see the awakening of England. Second, they are people of *passion*. David Brainard, ministering in the dynamic days of the First Great Awakening, became a missionary to the American Indians. He was so concerned for the conversion of the lost that he said: "I cared not where or how I lived, or what hardships I went through, so that I could but gain souls to Christ. While I was asleep I dreamed of these things, and when I awoke the first thing I thought of was this great work. All my desire was for the conversion of the heathen, and all my hope was in God."[10] He died at the age of 30, pouring out his very life for the salvation of others. Revival develops that type of spirit. Moreover, revival demands people of great spiritual *power*. Never was there a more powerful preacher than Charles Haddon Spurgeon. Multitudes came to Christ as the British people hung on his words during the days of the British revival of 1858-60. In the final analysis, the prophets used in revival are people of purpose, passion, power, and the presence of God.

The Mobilization of the Laity

The eighth principle of revival gears laymen for ministry. It is not only great prophetic leaders but also the lay people who are profoundly involved during revival. Pastors have challenged, pleaded, and even begged their lay folks to give their time and energies in service, particularly for the saving of the lost. Still, the majority of laity are merely passive spectators. We should be thankful to God for the faithful few who do respond, but there are so few. These few will never turn the blitz of Satan as the "few" in the battle of Britain who turned to the Nazi tide in World War II.

If we are to see world evangelization, all the people of God must get into the warfare. When an awakening arrives, the whole company of Christians are so revived and set afire that service for Christ abounds everywhere.

Every great spiritual awakening is testimony to this principle. The Asbury students went witnessing and testifying completely across the nation. The Welsh laity became great witnesses. Every revived American frontiersman became an evangelist. The illustrations are endless. We shall probably never see the multitude of laypeople motivated, enlisted, equipped, and sent out in ministry until an awakening comes. When God revives His people, evangelism naturally flows through the lives of those in His awakened church.

Ebb and Flow

Finally, there is a principle of ebb and flow in all revivals. Revivals come, and then they pass away. The situation today finds us at the ebb time. It seems we are in desperate need of a spiritual awakening at the immediate moment.

Key Words for Spiritual Awakening

Three key words emerge in answer to the question, "When will spiritual awakening come?"

Challenge

The first word is *challenge*. People need to be challenged. Then they challenge others to seek a genuine awakening. It is important to permit the Spirit of God to speak and challenge us, then in turn to challenge others, as God is sought in revival.

The Bible

The second key word involves the Scriptures. God always uses His holy Word in revival. The Bible makes a three-fold impact in reviving times. First of all, it convicts people of personal sin and the need for cleansing. Secondly, the Scriptures help us acknowledge the absolute lordship of Jesus Christ in everyday life. Personal commitment is the core of revival. Finally, the Bible gives guidelines on how to attain true spiritual power in the fullness of the Holy Spirit.

Prayer

The last key word in revival is *intercessory prayer.* Investigate every great spiritual awakening beginning with the Bible, moving through church history, and proceeding to the present moment. Fervent prayer is always a bottom line. In the First Great Awakening the ardent prayers of Jonathan Edwards and others brought the blessings. The Second Great Awakening came as a direct result of the call of the "Concert of Prayer." The Prayer Revival of 1858 became itself a prayer revival. The Korean church goes forward today on the wings of prayer. The most significant action Christians can take to bring about an awakening is to band together in prayer groups, study God's Word, and fervently pray that the Lord will rend the heavens. Matthew Henry said, "When the Lord is about to pour out unusual mercies, He first of all sets His people a-praying."[11]

Intercessory Prayer

How should Christians pray? Christians should earnestly pray for the Spirit of prayer. Apart from the strength and power of the Holy Spirit there is never vital, dynamic prayer. Perhaps people need to pray to pray. Christians are to pray for a spiritual awakening specifically. Most pray regularly and sincerely, but often we ask for everything except revival. Most have been in evangelistic crusades and in countless prayer meetings for such efforts and are constantly being urged to pray for the "revival." The people will pray for everything except for that which they are gathered.

Charles G. Finney tells of one dedicated woman who became so burdened and anxious for the unconverted that she devoted herself to prayer for their salvation in a most sacrificial manner. Her distress and anxiety heightened until she pleaded with her pastor to call a special meeting to reach the lost. The pastor put her off, he felt no such concern. She persisted—so did he. Finally, she came to him and said, "If you do not appoint a meeting I shall die, for there is going to certainly be a revival." He relented and the next Sunday invited all who might be concerned for their salvation to a special meeting to seek God. He did not know of one concerned person, but to his amazement an unbelievable number responded. How did this dear woman know? The secret of the Lord was with her. An agonizing prayer burden brings awakenings.

Real praying calls for real sacrifice. Finney noted that an awakening comes when Christians are willing to make the necessary sacrifices to carry it on. The reality must be faced that sacrifices are often great. It will cost time and energy. It can cost reputation and material gain. People will be baffled; some will even be resistant. One must be willing to forfeit his respect among the world's crowd. God will now allow any limits to be imposed. If Christians hold back their time, efforts, image, or anything, the Holy Spirit will be grieved and the awakening will end.

It has become clear that the divine mix that always seems to ferment revival is a desperate need, a willing God who is providentially maneuvering circumstances to a climax, and a dedicated handful of prevailing prayer warriors who will intercede until the revival dawns. In a word, a spiritual praying band and the sovereignty of God forms the warp and woof of an awakening. That receipt provides bread for the hungry.

And when revival comes, evangelism flourishes. If this nation of ours is ever to be brought to the foot of the cross once more, it is time for a revival. Therefore won't you dedicate yourself to intercessory prayer for a great spiritual awakening? It could be that God would have you to gather about yourself a praying band to intercede for a great revival.

Conclusion

There is a story that provides a beautiful illustration of what a small handful of praying people can accomplish as they pray for genuine revival. On the island of Lewis in the Hebrides Islands, off the northwest coast of Scotland, in 1949, a spiritual sterility had settled into the whole archipelago. The churches were dead and sparsely attended. Secular humanism and materialism dominated the mindset of the entire population. There were, however, a handful of burdened believers. Half a dozen men had been gathering outside their little village on the island of Lewis in a barn several nights of the week interceding for revival. Many times their fervent prayers extended unto the early hours of the morning. This had been going on for some months. One night, in the midst of their fervent prayers, one of the younger men sat up and said, "Men, this is so much rubbish. Could it be that we, the very ones who are most concerned for revival, are the very ones who are standing in this way? God has laid upon my heart a passage of Scripture: 'Who shall ascend to the hill of the Lord? And who shall stand in his holy place? He who has clean hands and a pure heart' (Psalm 24:3-4)." These words brought them under deep conviction of their own sins. They were literally prostrated to the dirt floor of the barn. They cried out to God in an agony of confession and repentance. Then after all their sins had been confessed, the Lord poured the glory of the Holy Spirit upon them and they were virtually lifted to heaven itself.

After the revived band was able to compose itself, the members made their way back into the village. By now it was early morning. Much to their surprise, when they entered their small community, they found lights on in all the houses. The entire population was up, dressed, and gathered at the police station. They thought some tragedy had occurred. But on inquiring they discovered that at the same moment the Spirit of God had fallen upon them in the barn in convicting power, He had also fallen upon all the lost people of the community, awakened them up out of their sleep, and being so convicted they were unable to get back to sleep. So they dressed and gathered at the police station trying to find someone to tell them how to be saved. As can be imagined, before dawn actually broke upon the community, practically the entire population had come to faith in Jesus Christ.

That is revival; that is what a praying band can accomplish; and that is how great evangelism will take place. Will *you* be part of a praying band in your community to see God do great things of righteousness and salvation in your midst?

Notes

1. Mendel Taylor, *Exploring Evangelism* (Kansas City: Beacon Hill Press, 1964), 409.

2. Lewis A. Drummond, *The Awakening That Must Come* (Nashville: Broadman Press, 1978), 103.

3. Ryken LeLand, *Worldly Saints—The Puritans As They Really Were* (Grand Rapids: Academic Books, Zondervan Publishing House, 1986).

4. *The Journal of John Wesley,* cited in Lewis A. Drummond, *The Awakening That Must Come*, 85.

5. Ibid.

6. Film by Campus Crusade for Christ, International, narrated by J. Edwin Orr, Arrowhead Springs, California.

7. Ibid.

8. Drummond, *The Awakening That Must Come*, 17-18.

9. James Beems, *Revivals: Their Laws and Leaders* (Grand Rapids: Baker Book House, 1960).

10. Drummond, *The Awakening That Must Come*, 92.

11. Film by Campus Crusade for Christ, International, Arrowhead Springs, California.

11 | Evangelism: Its Primacy and Organization in the Local Church
Larry L. Lewis

Remember that oldtime religion? I certainly do. I remember the hot August nights when we all sang the familiar evangelistic hymns of our faith. I remember the joyful celebration when sinners fell sway to the Spirit of God and gave their hearts to Jesus. We rejoiced when we watched as they were baptized. Sometimes the whole town was affected by our church's revival meeting.

Whatever happened to those days? In reality, they probably were not as good as we remember them. We remember the days when people came to revivals and were saved, but we forget that we probably worked a little harder then. We weren't as busy with other things. Our world ran a little slower, and we made time for cottage prayer meetings, for pack-a-pew nights and for two-week meetings. Today it seems many people don't have the time for such a commitment.

However, there are churches across the nation that have discovered ways to reach people for Christ even though we live in a rushed society. The simultaneous revival crusades nationwide proved that people can be reached with the gospel, and can still be brought to worship centers to hear the gospel preached. It is important to analyze how churches do make evangelism a priority and to discover what it means to have an evangelistic church.

Right Attitude

Priorities need to be established. Realizing that evangelism is the fuel that makes a church go, helps to put proper perspective on the task of the church. No one can deny that an effective antidote for a sagging church spirit is seeing people saved. It is very effective in resurrecting a dead church and turning around a declining church.

First, a church must decide that it wants to be evangelistic above all else. It cannot separate missions and ministry from evangelism. Rather, it must do missions evangelistically. When the church involves itself in ministry, it should do so evangelistically. Every activity in the church must lend itself to evangelism. Everything from feeding the poor in the community to choir tours by the youth, must bear the stamp of evangelism. Otherwise, the church has little reason for being.

One of the best ways to create the right attitude toward evangelism in the church is by creating a climate that will enable evangelism to happen. This will require a concerted effort. Churches have traditionally depended on the Sunday School to carry the burden of evangelism for the church. Depending on the commitment of individual Sunday School teachers, leaders, and officers, this has worked with some success. Many pastors will testify that the Sunday School is a most effective tool for reaching the lost. Chances are the pastors who feel strongly about Sunday School are promoting evangelism in other ways as well. There can be problems with placing the burden of evangelism on one single program of work.

A church cannot rely on one single program of work to do all that needs to be done in evangelism. Most denominations have more than one program to assist churches in evangelism. Denominations that have mission boards for home missions often establish at least three programs of work to help churches become more evangelistic: mass evangelism, personal evangelism and evangelism development.

Denominational programs emphasize evangelism in all the major programs of a church (Bible study or Sunday School, Discipleship Training, etc.). Remember, simply emphasizing and promoting the work of evangelism is not enough. Specific strategies must be developed to reach the lost. Churches need an evangelism council to carry out the work of evangelism. The evangelism council is responsible for creating a climate in the church for evangelism and for developing specific evangelistic strategies to involve every church member in the process of sharing Jesus Christ with a lost world.

Even a small church can have a church evangelism council. The pastor and a dedicated layperson who has a vision for reaching the lost can work together to formulate specific strategies for evangelism in the church. Many programs are offered by denominational agencies to help churches with their evangelistic planning. Denominational directors of evangelism in regional and state convention or conferences have information on evangelistic strategy planning and materials to help every church.

If a church is larger, the evangelism council can be composed of persons who help formulate strategies in specific areas of work. The council should have an evangelism director who plans with the council and who represents the work of evangelism to the larger planning body of the church. A mass evangelism director and a personal evangelism director serve on the evangelism council to represent specific evangelistic strategies in these two areas. In much larger churches, evangelism specialists are added to the council to enable it to do better planning.

The charts on the following page describe graphically the two organizations available to churches. The basic organization for smaller churches and the expanded church evangelism council for larger churches are displayed in these two charts.

With the basic organization the chart describes, a church can begin to plan for specific evangelistic strategies. Revivals and other soul-winning training events can be planned under the leadership of the council. Specific events and special partnership activities can be planned through the church program organizations of the church.

The evangelism council should allow a great deal time for planning with the other programs of work in the church to emphasize evangelism. The evangelism council should serve as the conscience of the church in everything it does. It should continually ask, "Who will be reached with the gospel of Jesus Christ by this project?"

The evangelism council should unashamedly ask every organization to participate 100 percent in activities and programs that seek to bring people to Jesus. Goals should be set and shared with the church. If evangelism is not planned for and shared with the church, people will not be reached as effectively as they could be.

Chart I: **BASIC ORGANIZATION**

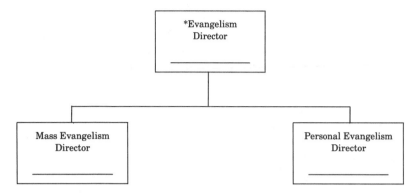

*The director of the Church Evangelism Council should be a member of the church council. If the pastor chooses to be director of the Church Evangelism Council, either the Mass or Personal Evangelism director should be on the church council to represent evangelism.

Chart II: **EXPANDED ORGANIZATION**

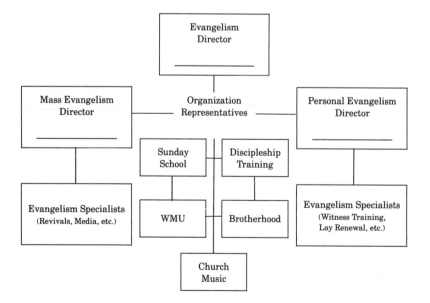

The Role of the Pastor

Pastors seem to be inundated with information and strategies related to the work of the church, because they are the key to the development of church programs. To develop a mission-minded church, the pastor must be for missions. If he is not a personal evangelist himself, winning people to Christ will be a byproduct of the church's ministry and not its key function. Even though pastors cannot do everything, they certainly can set the direction and tone of what is done in the church. Pastors should help create an atmosphere within the church that is conducive to evangelism. The pastor's support of evangelistic strategies developed by the evangelism council is vital. He must be involved in those strategies, but not try to do all the work himself. The pastor can add a flavor of optimism and excitement to what the council plans to do by letting the church know of his support. Whether it be preparing for revival or leading the church in an evangelistic ministry program to the community, the pastor is an important motivator for action.

The pastor should work closely with the church evangelism council to encourage members to dream of evangelistic possibilities. The pastor should involve persons on the council who have an evangelistic spirit and who are creative people. If the pastor thinks creatively about the kinds of people who should be on the council, much of his work will be achieved as these evangelistically minded people plan together.

Once the church has been organized for evangelism by establishing an evangelism council, work can begin. The pastor should prepare the church for the strategies that will come from the council. A series of several evangelistic messages preached by the pastor will begin to set the stage for evangelism planning in the church. Helpful aids such as posters, training materials, evangelistic tracts, and brochures should appear around the church.

Sunday School teachers and all leaders of the church organizations should be challenged to begin focusing on evangelism. The pastor may need to give some training to these leaders on how to share their faith or how to make a witnessing visit in the home.

One of the most dramatic ways to begin the work of evangelism in a church is by launching evangelistic strategies for a "soul-winning commitment day." By observing a soul-winning commitment day, a church can formally announce to the members and to the community that the year is going to be characterized by an emphasis on evangelism. Members are asked to make commitments to become personal witnesses. If the pastor will emphasize the importance of Soul-Winning Commitment Day, the work of the evangelism council will become a natural outgrowth of the commitments made on that day.

Planning for Mass Evangelism

Strategy planning is not limited to projects that can be done through Sunday School or Discipleship Training only. A major portion of the work of the evangelism council should be devoted to planning mass evangelism events.

Mass evangelism events include: revival crusades in the church, local or area crusades, citywide crusades, associational simultaneous revivals, nationwide simultaneous revivals, or involvement in a very large campaign such as a Billy Graham Crusade. Wherever masses of people gather to hear the gospel, mass evangelism occurs. The mass evangelism director leads the way in helping the pastor and the council plan for such events.

Revival crusades need to be carefully planned in order to succeed. Our society has changed dramatically from the days when the church was the center of social activity. People have hundreds of other places to go that compete with the church for their attention and free time. For a revival to be a harvest of souls and rekindling of commitment by Christians, plans have to be made. The Holy Spirit honors our faithfulness in planning. Planning never hinders the work of the Spirit; planning enhances what the Spirit wants to do.

Jesus knew the value of planning. He made detailed plans for all he did. An example is the upperroom supper with His disciples. He made detailed plans for that meal. He even had others involved in those plans. It was not a spontaneous event, but a meal Jesus made preparation for. Revivals must also be planned well to be successful.

The evangelism council initiates the planning. It can serve as the committee to make plans for the revival. Others can be brought on the council temporarily to aid in the planning. Items such as publicity, pre-revival prayer services, transportation needs, attendance building plans, special events, and special nights can be handled by the council. Involve as many people in the church as is practical. Attempt to give every church member something to do in preparation for the revival. If people are accountable to the council, the pastor, and most of all, to the Lord, they will be faithful to the revival services. Ask the people for commitment.

Take advantage of the value of advertisement. Local newspapers, radio and television spots, paid ads, circulars, and letters to church members are valuable aids in preparation for the revival.

The most important thing that should be done in preparation for revival is gathering a prospect list. People are considered prospects once you have a name, location or address, phone number, and strategy for getting that person to the church.

Survey church rolls. Look for extended family members who are unchurched. These people often go unnoticed. Survey the community. It is not biblical to develop strategies for reaching people that do not include the community or neighborhood under the shadow of the church steeple. God cannot bless a church that practices selective evangelism.

Many other strategies and plans can be developed that will enhance the success of mass evangelism events. Special materials are available from most denominational agencies for evangelism that help churches develop mass evangelism strategies.

Planning for Personal Evangelism

Personal evangelism must be the most important emphasis of the church. If a church is filled with members who do not practice personal evangelism, the church will never change the community for Christ. Personal evangelism does not take place naturally. Here is where the devil practices most of his influence over the lives of Christians. He doesn't want Christians to witness. He tells them that it is not necessary; that it is too hard; and that is the task of the preacher.

Personal evangelism training involves two things: actual training and encouragement. Church members must be trained to verbally share their faith with others. A lot of materials are available that can aid in this training. Denominational mission boards publish tracts, booklets, and manuals that can be used in churches to enable members to share Jesus with the lost. Many other evangelical organizations and agencies do the same.

Programs such as Continuing Witness Training (CWT) and Evangelism Explosion (EE) stress the use of memorized presentations of the gospel. Church members train in the classroom but also go on witnessing visits so they can put their training into action. Apprentices are trained by others who are already equipped to share their faith. Both EE and CWT are designed to continue the process of training and equipping witnesses in the local church.

Lay Evangelism Schools (LES) are also helpful in teaching church members to share their faith. Groups of churches, such as Baptist associations or Methodist conferences, can join together in conducting an LES to enable large groups to be trained for witnessing. LES's are also effective in preparation for revival crusades because church members are trained to reach others through practical experience with witnessing.

Regardless of the method used, churches should make personal evangelism central to all the church activities. Those who visit for the church should do so with the objective of leading the person being visited to faith in Christ. Sunday School visitation or prospect discovery should be evangelistic. Hospital visitation should be evangelistic. Church members should learn to feel at home sharing their faith as a normal routine when they visit. Pastors should regularly preach and teach on personal evangelism, but most of all, pastors should *model, model, model personal evangelism.*

Many people believe that pastors are personal evangelists naturally. However, some pastors, by their own admission, have not witnessed in a long time. Some report weeks going by without a witnessing encounter. Obviously, pastors are busy. Administrative duties and maintenance of the programs of the church take enormous blocks of time, but the church will put first what the pastor puts first. If personal evangelism is the pastor's priority, it can become the priority of the church.

Developing a comprehensive approach to evangelism in the local church takes commitment. It takes work. It means that plans will have to be made. Obviously the Holy Spirit leads the way, and the Holy Spirit is the one who convicts, calls, and regenerates the unsaved. Church members must realize that planting the seed of God's Word and watering and nurturing those seed is part of the process of evangelism. That opens the way for the Holy Spirit to work, and we reap the harvest of souls. That is the real business of the church.

12 | Training for Evangelism (Formal and Informal)
Chuck Kelley

There are many issues involved when considering evangelism. A major factor for a successful evangelistic program is proper training of the eager individuals who want to be involved. How do you prepare people to do the work of evangelism? Inadequate skills breed discouragement in any worker. Enthusiasm and zeal fade from those who have a vision but don't know where or how to get started. All attempts to enhance the involvement of persons in evangelism without adequate training are doomed to failure.

Southern Baptists, as a whole, need to seriously consider the issue of evangelism training. Statistics on baptisms for the nation's largest Protestant denomination were flat for a number of years and declining from 1982 to 1985. Perhaps one of the reasons is found in the Home Mission Board's discovery that less than 20 percent of all Southern Baptist churches spent as much as ten hours in 1983 training church members to share their faith. It is one thing to give people a burden about evangelism. It is quite another to give them the tools to do something about that burden.

People can be equipped for the work of evangelism in a variety of ways. Approaches to evangelism training are determined by such factors as the type of evangelism to be done, the people to be involved, and the circumstances to be faced. Following is a description of the general characteristics which should be present in any evangelism training process. Attention will be given to both formal and informal aspects of equipping persons to share their faith. Formal aspects of training will refer to those matters which can take place in a group or class setting. Informal matters will include those matters which cannot take place in a group or class setting.

Heart-Centered

The Book of Acts pulsates with the fire and zeal of the evangelistic witness of the early church. The key to understanding the passion of their testimony is found in Acts 4:20. Peter and John were arrested and threatened for healing and preaching in the name of Jesus. When commanded not to preach in the name of Jesus again, they responded, "We cannot but speak the things which we have seen and heard" (KJV). Their evangelism was a result of their personal life with Jesus. Evangelism is sterile and artificial unless it flows from a burning heart. All the training in the world will not overcome the inertia of a disobedient faith.

Proverbs 4:23 advises, "Keep thy heart with all diligence; for out of it are the issues of life" (KJV). This is not a reference to the organ of our body which pumps our blood. It speaks of the center of our emotions and will. As we believe and feel, we will act. When we daily experience the presence and power of Jesus, we will speak of Him to others. Moviemakers have discovered the secret to a hit movie is not a well conceived, expensively produced, widely distributed advertising campaign. A hit movie is the result of, what Hollywood calls, WOM. The abbreviation stands for word of mouth. What counts at the box office is what people tell their friends.

The implications for evangelism are obvious. Evangelism training does not start with teaching skills in how to witness. It must start with helping Christians discover how to have a meaningful life with God. Teaching techniques for evangelism to Christians who do not have a dynamic, satisfying relationship with Jesus, is similar to giving someone the keys to a car without a battery. Knowledge about driving is irrelevant, for the engine will not start until energy is present. Evangelism training must deal with one's relationship with God. When that is right, a person will find a way to witness. Training then becomes a way to sharpen and refine the natural and spontaneous witness of a heart in love with God.

Spirit-Empowered

Imagine receiving the gift of a Rolls-Royce. The beautiful, expensive car is given to you for your use at no cost. You jump into it excited and ready to go for your first ride, only to discover the gas tank is empty. Engineering, craftsmanship, and luxury are meaningless without fuel to provide the power. The Holy Spirit provides the "gas" for witnessing. Through His divine presence and power, believers are energized to share their faith with others.

An effective evangelism training program will breed a sense of dependency upon the Holy Spirit. It is not enough to know the Holy Spirit is essential for sharing the gospel. The witness must have a conscious sense of the Spirit's presence and power. I suppose one of the most common prayers offered on visitation night is "Lord, let no one be home when I knock!" That kind of fear is common but unnecessary. According to Acts 1:8, the Holy Spirit brings power into our lives. In John 14:16-17, Jesus said the Spirit is always with us, providing encouragement and comfort. The presence of the Holy Spirit removes the requirement for natural skills in order to witness. Through His supernatural power, the Holy Spirit makes witnessing a possibility and responsibility for every believer. Any process for equipping persons to witness should include help for recognizing the Spirit's presence and experiencing the Spirit's power.

There is another reason to train persons for Spirit-empowered witnessing. Apart from the Holy Spirit there is no regeneration of the sinful heart. One who witnesses in the strength of human skills will have human results. The Holy Spirit alone can convince a person of the reality of his or her sin, God's righteousness, and the coming judgment (John 16:7-11). Persuasive people may get decisions, but the Holy Spirit brings about conversion. The story is told of a drunk who stopped D. L. Moody on a street one night. He told the famous evangelist, "I am one of your converts." Moody is said to have replied, "You must be one of mine. You are certainly not one of God's." Evangelism must be done in the power of the Holy Spirit if genuine conversions are to result.

Skill-Intensive

There is a time and place for the academic study of evangelism. However, the development of specific skills in presenting the gospel is a more critical need than developing an understanding of the field of evangelism. An academic study of evangelism is only appropriate in conjunction with the development of practical skills. The students in our seminary are all required to take a course which teaches them how to witness to lost people. That course was developed after a survey revealed the majority of the class rarely witnessed and felt a real sense of fear about doing personal evangelism. The seminary students had a greater need for specific skills in witnessing than they did for knowledge about the field of evangelism. Most Christians are in a similar position. Theological education and church programming should make equipping persons to actually do the work of evangelism a primary priority.

The basic skills needed for evangelism are simple. Christians need to know how to tell others what Jesus Christ has done in their lives. They also need to be able to share the gospel and explain to a lost person how to be saved. With that basic knowledge, any believer should be able to lead a person to salvation through faith in Christ. Other skills would be helpful. Learning how to start to make a transition into a spiritual conversation, how to adapt a gospel presentation to specific persons or situations, and how to handle questions or objections would be very useful. The particular skills emphasized in the training process will reflect the type of evangelism to be done. Whatever form evangelism training takes, skill development should be a primary concern.

Field-Based

Evangelism training should also be field-based. There must be actual witness encounters with lost people if the process is to be effective. No seminary receives accreditation from the Association of Theological Schools unless its curriculum includes some sort of field education. Professional educators recognize the classroom at best offers only a partial view of what the real world is actually like. Learning is incomplete until knowledge has been applied to specific situations. This principle is particularly true in regard to evangelism. All the characteristics discussed above are formal aspects of evangelism training. To at least some extent, they can be taught in the formal setting of a class or group session. The best classroom for evangelism, however, is a conversation with a lost person. An effective training program will get participants out of the classroom and into dialogue with unbelievers.

One main reason that most people give for not witnessing more often is fear. A field-based program is essential for helping persons replace fear with confidence in themselves as witnesses. I have found confidence in witnessing to be a result of training, practice, and experience. Training is the explanation and discussion of how witnessing is done. Practice is going through the process in a controlled environment. Experience is actually sharing the gospel with a lost person. Consider the example of a football team. The coach will begin with an explanation of how to block and tackle. The explanation is followed by players practicing what they learned on other team members. The players practice blocking and tackling one another over and over until they are comfortable with the process. Experience follows as the team plays a game against an opponent, applying what was learned in the pressure of an actual game. A football player gains confidence when he has training, practice, and experience.

Evangelism training which seeks to develop confident witnesses will incorporate the same process. There must be training sessions when Christians are taught how to witness. There must be time for practice when the group can act out what they have learned in a controlled environment. They must share with one another, or other Christians, over and over until they are comfortable talking about their faith. Ultimately, there must be an actual experience of sharing the gospel with a lost person. Confidence comes from discovering that what has been learned works in the real world of actual experience.

Results-Oriented

Persons are trained to witness so that they might lead others to Christ. The role of education in evangelism is often thought to be that of giving students a thorough understanding. That is an inadequate conception in regard to evangelism. The Greek word we translate "evangelism" means an announcement of good news. The New Testament regularly uses it in the context of calling for a response to that good news. When John the Baptist announced his good news he called his hearers to repent. Evangelism always seeks results, and that expectation should be expressed in the training process. A results-oriented approach to witness training will transfer the desire for reaping a spiritual harvest to the trainee.

The best evangelism training programs do not wait until after participants are trained for results. The reaping of a harvest is part of the training process. Designing field experiences during the training is an expression of the harvest mentality. All results, positive and negative, should be shared with the training group. In this way participants will learn their witnessing does result in changed lives. Not all persons visited during the training process will be born again, but some will. The public sharing of witness results shows trainees the sowing, cultivating, and harvesting process which is evangelism. Christians must be trained to recognize that the goal, the purpose, and the expectation of every effort in evangelism is the conversion of the lost.

Anyone who witnesses will experience both success and failure in seeing persons accept Christ as their Savior. Some lost persons will be responsive to the Spirit's wooing while others will not. The trainee needs to learn that reality so he will not be overly discouraged by failure nor made overly prideful by success.

Conclusion

Evangelism training must be the major task of this generation of believers. The early church exploded across the ancient world because the first Christians went everywhere speaking of Jesus. The contemporary church will also explode when it recaptures the evangelistic zeal of those first-century believers. In an attempt to make that explosion a reality, training in evangelism, both formal and informal, should become a standard procedure in the local church as well as in Christian colleges and seminaries. As Christians learn to articulate their faith to others, their faith will become more meaningful to themselves. The battle cry of this generation of the church must become "Every Believer a Witness!"

The best strategy for evangelism training has not yet been developed, and it never will. Many different strategies are effective and appropriate. The approach each Christian takes should reflect personal needs and circumstances. However, any approach used should be heart-centered, Spirit-empowered, skill-intensive, field-based, and results-oriented. Jack Stanton has marked a path for all of us to follow. Evangelism must be the top priority of the church. Believers must be trained to share their faith.

13 | The Role of the Vocational Evangelist

Leonard Sanderson

In Southern Baptist preacher parlance, the vocational evangelist is the leader of evangelistic events, commonly called revivals. The word *evangelist* occurs three times in the New Testament (Acts 21:8; Eph. 4:11; 2 Tim. 4:5) and means "one who announces the good news." Obviously its meaning cannot be separated form the Greek root word which is translated "preach the gospel," "bring good tiding," or "announce the gospel." The New Testament word *evangelist* suggests that this person is one who tells others the good news with a purpose of making them disciples of Jesus Christ. The word *vocational* has been used in recent years in preference to *full-time, free-lance, professional,* or *independent.* The reason for the qualifying word is that many evangelists do not "make a living" as evangelists. Not only is every pastor to "do the work of an evangelist" (2 Tim. 4:5), even though he is not "full-time," but every Christian is to "make disciples." So the modifier, "vocational," is necessary.

According to Paul (Eph. 4:11), the evangelist is a church officer, along with apostles, prophets, pastors, and teachers. Christ's objective in gifting people for all these offices is perfecting the saints for the work of building up the body of Christ in the manner described in the verses that follow (vv. 13-16). So the evangelist, while a specialist, is interested in the health and well-being of the total body (the church).

As a Christian Person

While the title of this chapter may imply what the evangelist *does*, discussion begins with who the evangelist *is*. The first direct reference to an "evangelist" in the New Testament is Philip, and the first information about Philip is in regard to his personal life. He was a man of good reputation, full of the Spirit, and wisdom (Acts 6:3). His behavior reveals even more concerning his spiritual maturity. His ministry in Samaria exhibited a superior understanding of the message and ministry of Jesus in Philip's desire to give the gospel to all people (Acts 8:5). He also demonstrated the quality of the Holy Spirit's control in his life by recognizing and following the Holy Spirit's leadership (8:26,29) in personal witnessing. The first and most important characteristic of the vocational evangelist has to do with his personal relationship with God.

Complete commitment to Christ is a daily need. The evangelist, of all people, must be a new creation. To be an effective preacher of the good news a person must meet all the conditions of cross-bearing which Jesus commanded (Matt. 10:38; 16:24; Mark 10:21). Every day of his life the vocational evangelist needs the resolution and commitment of Paul: "I am crucified with Christ: nevertheless I live; yet not I, but Christ liveth in me: and the life which I now live in the flesh I live by the faith of the Son of God, who loved me, and gave himself for me" (Gal. 2:20, KJV). This need is probably more intensified for the evangelist. Every servant of Jesus Christ, professional and non-professional, has needs peculiar to his own life and ministry. In some ways the vocational evangelist may be uncommonly vulnerable to certain pressures.

Family pressures

It is a well-known reality that vocational evangelists are away from home and family more than other church leaders. Foreign missionaries are separated from their extended families; but, if they are married, their spouses and children are near them. Most pastors get less family time than most other people, but they do see and are seen almost daily by family members. Denominational leaders are away from home more than local church pastors and staff, but they usually have more total prime relaxation time with family. Many vocational evangelists are away from home and family more than half the time; some as much as forty weeks of the year. This exceeds the away-from-home time by military people (except in time of war), salespeople, others whose vocations have similar requirements. Most people whose vocations keep them away from home for weeks or months at a time also have weeks or months when they are almost totally at home. Busy evangelists do not enjoy that luxury.

Of all the pressures of the vocational evangelist, living away from home is the worst. However, the other extreme has its ramifications. Being home too much is even worse. One man who had been a vocational evangelist about a year said, "I have worn out the grass in the yard going to the mailbox, the carpet in the den walking the floor; and the knees of my pants in prayer." If wives and children worry about the absence of the husband and father, think of how they worry when the invitations run thin. Evangelists and their families need to be strong in the Lord.

Pressures from the People

Typically, the evangelist enjoys outstanding relationships with people. He associates with the best people in the world: pastors, church staff members, and the very choicest Christians in every city and community. The praise, accolades, applause, compliments, affirmations, acclamations, and felicitations abound day after day. This provides needful encouragement, strength, renewal, and challenge. It also provokes vanity, pride, embarrassment, and guilt. However, there are those times long and loathsome, when applause, acclaim, and accolades are not seen, heard, or even felt. Those are the days when an evangelist considers becoming a pastor, staff person, or furniture salesman. Those are the nights when he calls his wife just to get her affirmation, or refrains in order to protect her.

George A. Buttrick tells how low he felt one day following a terrible sermon. There were no compliments as he stood at the door and shook hands. Finally, one woman, the last person out the door said, "Thank you, pastor, for your sermon." He responded, "Thank you, but it was too long." The smiling lady said, "No, it just seemed long." Evangelists need to be strong in the Lord. Most importantly, the Lord has the right to expect that of us. So do the people.

Financial Pressures

Sometimes evangelists are criticized because they are making too much money. An inactive deacon asked a customer in his business, "Do you know how much money the evangelistic team took out of our town?" "No," answered the customer, "but I know how much I gave to support the gospel ministry in some places where they cannot pay their own way."

Once a member of the finance committee said to a pastor, "We have had some complaints about how much we gave the evangelist." The pastor asked, "Was the complaint by somebody who gave or somebody who didn't give? It was all voluntary."

Obviously, many criticisms are ludicrous. However, it is essential, for the sake of the gospel, the evangelist be above reproach in money matters. For this reason, Billy Graham and many other evangelists have organized non-profit corporations which have elected directors or board members to handle matters of finance. All honoraria, gifts, fees and contributions are deposited with the association and the evangelist receives a salary like a pastor or denominational person. Even with that precaution, evangelists should be good personal stewards of money, as well as time and talents. Evangelists need to be strong in the Lord.

Success Pressures

Vocational evangelists are especially vulnerable to the old truism "Nothing succeeds like success." Good reports, good recommendations, good impressions and good exposure are things revival invitations are made of. Therefore, evangelists are tempted to exaggerate and are often accused of yielding to the temptation. Evangelists need to be strong in the Lord.

As Personal Witness

I learned more about personal evangelism from Norris Gilliam than any other person. It began in 1945. I was pastor in Tennessee while in seminary, and Gilliam came to lead a revival. I met the train ten miles away. When we got into my car, he asked about the looseleaf notebook in the front seat. I explained, "These are our evangelistic prospects." "How many?" he asked. I told him there were about 300. He asked if any lived between the train station and the hotel. When I answered affirmatively, he suggested we start seeing them. We knocked on doors and witnessed until time for the Monday evening service without checking into the hotel or eating dinner. For two weeks we began each morning at 9:00 visiting prospects until 12:00, allowed him to rest from 1:00 till 2:00 (I was so glad), and beginning at 2:00, we visited until time for the services.

Together, during two weeks, we witnessed to more than 150 persons, and more than 50 of them were baptized during the revival. Perhaps I have usually not been that diligent, but I know scores of times when the evangelistic revival began with the personal work of pastor and evangelist. It is certainly a good launching pad for teaching and leading church members in witnessing.

Jesus practiced personal witnessing in the presence of his disciples, then sent them out. He heard their reports, continued to teach them, allowed them to watch Him again, and sent them back out.

Paul practiced personal witnessing and taught it to his evangelistic students and helpers (Acts 20:20; 1 Tim. 4:14; 2 Tim. 1:7; 2:2; 4:5). He had been called to this work and declared that he was not disobedient (Acts 26:16-20). His work in Philippi illustrates his personal evangelistic work (Acts 16:14-15, 31-32).

John Wesley taught his preachers, "You have nothing to do but save souls. You are not to preach so many times, or take care of this or that society, but to save as many souls as you can." Billy Graham has repeatedly said that personal evangelism is the most effective method of evangelism. To listen to his preaching is to be reminded of how much this busy man engages in personal witnessing.

As Church Builder

Paul's reminder in Ephesians 4:11-17 is sufficient to convince every serious evangelist and pastor that the evangelist is a church officer with responsibility for building the church qualitatively as well as quantitatively. Evangelism is decidedly indispensable in building the body of Christ. The evangelist's principal contribution to church-building is unmistakably the personal proclamation of the good news "publicly, and from house to house" (Acts 20:20, KJV). He is also responsible for leading the entire church in evangelism. However, the evangelist remembers he is only part of the body; not the head, but maybe the heart.

When I was asked to be evangelism director in Tennessee in 1953, I told the executive secretary I had no idea how to direct evangelism in a state convention. He answered, "You do it just like you do in your church." I explained that was my problem. In the church, all church organizations were involved in evangelism: the Sunday School in reaching people and teaching the Bible, the

Discipleship Training in training for evangelism, the Woman's Missionary Union and Brotherhood in doing personal evangelism, with youth and music and ministries vitally involved.

Vocational evangelists can encourage the pastor to include all the organizations in preparation for the evangelistic meeting. This way the revival begins among these very organizations, and they will keep it alive when the revival event is long past.

As Preacher

Pastoral preaching is the best preaching because the pastor identifies with the people and their needs better than anyone else. However, the vocational evangelist has some clear advantages. He has as much time for preparation as the pastor but can preach some of his best sermons in each church. He can focus on evangelistic or revival messages. His experiences, as well as his study and observation, provide ample illustrations. He has fewer mental and physical distractions. As already indicated, the evangelist has numerous heavy pressures, but they are not clearly identified with the local congregation. The denominational person or preacher-professor has some of the above advantages but not the opportunities for evangelistic focus the vocational evangelist has.

Furthermore the vocational evangelist has some advantages in spiritual preparation for preaching. He is often deprived of home and family. This can be frustrating to the point of devastation. If, however, by prayer and the power of the Spirit, he can defeat this, he can use those lonely hours as time spent with God. This can transform his life and ministry.

C. E. Matthews told me about having Hyman Appleman for revival in the early days of Appleman's evangelistic ministry. He said, "Old Hyman prayed every minute he wasn't preaching or doing personal witnessing. We would come into the church building between visits, and while I was returning telephone calls or attending to some personal matter, Appleman would be in some Sunday School classroom praying." There was no doubt God was using his preaching ministry.

Some vocational evangelists are extremely effective communicators. Examples in America are George Whitefield, Gilbert Tennent, Jonathan Edwards, Charles G. Finney, Dwight L. Moody, R. A. Torrey, J. Wilbur Chapman, and Billy Graham. In addition to Graham, there are in America and elsewhere outstanding preachers among vocational evangelists today. To name some would be to exclude others. Future generations will recognize some of them, and eternity will reveal even more.

Though not usually recognized for their scholarship, vocational evangelists must be above-average communicators to survive. In this vein, God has given me the opportunity in recent years to appeal to seminary students to improve the scholarship of evangelists. I have been insisting that the smart ones become evangelists and that the evangelistic ones become smart. When this occurs, some of the greatest preaching ever will be heard.

As Pastor's Ally

All Christians are members of the body of Christ. Paul appealed to Christian leaders to recognize the ministries of others (1 Cor. 1:10-13; 12:1-30) and then explained that the basis of this kind of cooperation is *agapē* love. Wheat farmers in the Midwest and cotton farmers in the South prepare the soil, plant the seeds and care for the crops. They may bring in harvesters with heavy equipment to gather in the harvest. There is no competition, but cooperation, for the sake of the harvest (1 Cor. 3:7-9). Pastors and evangelists are allies in answer to Christ's call to prayer for harvesters (Matt. 9:38).

Most pastors, when they invite vocational evangelists to their churches, ask them to make suggestions about revival preparation. The responsible evangelist responds by making preparation suggestions that not only help the revival, but also have residual value in the life and ministry of the church. Surveys have revealed that more than 80 percent of the people who make professions of faith in Graham crusades do so the first time they attend. This is the result of months of preparation. Similar procedures can be successful in the local church. The people who become Christians during the revival have been cultivated and watered by pastoral leadership and lay participation beforehand. C. E. Matthews contended more than 70 percent of revival success was in preparation. The pastor and evangelist are allies.

The evangelist builds up the church and encourages the pastor. If the evangelist observes that the pastor is a good personal witness, he should compliment him publicly. If the pastor, in his praying and ministry, demonstrates unusual caring and concern for his people, it should be noted. If the pastor has led in effective preparation, proper acknowledgment should be made. The church and pastor should be stronger after the revival.

Conclusion

The key words are *Christian commitment*. God calls special people to vocational evangelism, whether preacher, musician, organizer, writer, teacher, or promoter. The relationship is one of special trust, a unique stewardship. He calls those who qualify with the Spirit. No person in the world should be more dedicated to his calling than the evangelist. Eternal life for many hangs in the balance (Rom. 10:14-15).

No servant of God should be a more earnest student of the Word. We now have a few evangelists earning Doctor of Theology degrees. They should be the best preachers, the best Christians, the most humble, the most bold, the best pray-ers, and the most diligent workers.

A church employed a fund-raising company to help raise money for a building. When the expert moved in and set up temporary offices, the pastor tried to be a good host. Among other things, the pastor offered him the keys to his boat tied up nearby the lakeside in a marina. The pastor explained that he might like to fish, shrimp, ski, or just ride in the boat. The man gave this answer: "Thank you very much. That is most generous, and I want you to know I appreciate it. But I have a rule that I do all my recreation before I get to a church to work, after I leave, or maybe occasionally, I leave town for rest and recreation, but never while I am on the job." That is a great example for vocational evangelists.

The wise evangelist owes it to God, his family, and himself to reserve time for relaxation and good health habit. However, if he has more time for recreation than the average business or professional person, he should re-examine his priorities as well as his schedule. With sufficient time allowed for study, prayer, personal witnessing, and preaching, the vocational evangelist will probably be the busiest person he knows.

14 | Organizing for the Evangelistic Crusade

E. J. Daniels
Revised by Granville Watson

Successful Techniques in Soul-Winning

Some seek to discredit the value of organization and promotion of the Lord's work; they scoff at what they call "the machinery and mechanics." Mere organization, plans, and promotion will not bring revivals and save souls. The power of the Spirit must be present. There must be a proper balance of spiritual guidance and organizational development. God must work through Christians.

Sufficient emphasis on proper promotion and detail work is an absolute necessity if a protracted meeting is to become a genuine crusade, and if witnessing is to win souls. It is important to do more than just pray and have faith. If prayers are to be answered, if faith is to function, if results are expected, put feet under your prayers. Many crusades fail for lack of proper planning, preparation, promotion, and pushing.

This chapter will highlight some promotional plans. Not all of the ideas presented are original; but most have been implemented in churchwide and citywide campaigns.

The Beginning of a Crusade

Pastors and churches want to have some voice in the original planning stages of a crusade. Of course, only one or two can start the plans moving; but they should (Vision Committee) invite other pastors and church leaders, whose hearts are burdened for souls, to join them; and after prayer, increase the circle to include even more. Plan a meeting (Invitation Committee) to which all orthodox pastors and many key laymen are invited.

This larger group should appoint a committee to suggest the evangelist, the time, and the place. The members should be wise and prayerful, as they make their recommendations. Those who started the crusade idea (Nominating Committee), along with all interested pastors, should prayerfully select a general chairman to lead the campaign. This person's reputation should be above reproach, one sound in the faith, who believes in crusades, and loves souls. This leader should have evident leadership ability. The fact that he is general chairman should carry weight with those who will cooperate when the plans for the crusade begin to materialize.

Setting Up the Crusade Organization

The varied work necessary for the planning, promotion, and conduction of a successful crusade campaign requires scores, sometimes hundreds or even thousands of people, depending on the scope of the effort. The more people involved in the crusade, the more likely it is to be successful from a human standpoint. The best way to get people to work is through well-chosen committees which provide work opportunities for people with various talents. For example, with a music committee, you can enlist the cooperation of those with musical talents and interests, and focus their efforts through this committee. In the same manner, all of the various committees not only do the work, but also act as channels through which to enlist other available support.

The Invitation Committee

When a citywide crusade is planned, this committee should be selected as early as possible from the core of interested pastors and laymen who have a burden for the crusade. These persons should seek to enlist the cooperation of all the churches and pastors in the effort at once. If they wait to seek this cooperation after the crusade plans are well under way, they will find that many pastors will be resentful and will not cooperate. If they are enlisted early, they can have a part in the development and promotion of the crusade.

The Committees Needed

Here is a list of the necessary committees, once the Invitation Committee has done its work. I will discuss each committee later.

1. Steering Committee
2. Prayer Committee
3. Witness Committee
4. Publicity Committee
5. Special Groups Committee
6. Music Committee
7. People-Serving Committee
8. Attendance-Transportation Committee
9. Arrangements Committee
10. Community Involvement Committee
11. Finance Committee

Securing Committee Chairmen

The Nominating Committee has the responsibility of nominating the General Chairman and the ten committee chairmen. Each committee should be headed by a capable person who has the qualifications necessary to lead his committee to do its task. This person should have the same spiritual qualifications suggested for the general chairman. He should be adapted to the particular work of his committee, as far as it is possible.

It may be wise to place pastors at the heads of many of the committees, but do not overlook capable laymen and laywomen. For example, a consecrated layman with business ability could well be the chairman of the finance committee. A nurse and capable mother should be selected to lead the child-care committee.

In a citywide crusade in which many churches are cooperating, it is wise to select the committee chairman from the various churches, rather than too many from one church. Do not put an unworthy or incapable person as head of a committee just to pass the honors around.

Churches Select Committee Members

It is wise to have at least one member on each committee from each church; in some cases, more than one is required. These persons are the crusade's contact for this particular work in each cooperating church. The committee members should be selected by a joint meeting of the general chairman, the committee chairman, and the cooperating pastors. The pastors are needed to recommend their best members for the various committees.

If some churches cannot be represented, a mimeographed list of all committees should be sent to each pastor. He should appoint members of his church to the various committees and return the list to the general chairman. All committee members should be contacted and asked if they will serve. Those who do not wish to do so would be replaced. Of course this applies to committee chairmen, also. The principle given for choosing chairmen should hold good for selecting members of the various committees. No member should be assigned to any committee when it is evident that he or she has no qualifications for the job.

The Duties of the Committees

Many full-time evangelists have mimeographed complete instructions for all committees and send these copies to every committee chairman. (My own would fill a book; obviously, I can only mention a few of them here.) I will attempt to give only brief suggestions regarding the work of the various committees.

Steering Committee

The Steering Committee should be official and active no less than eight months prior to the crusade date. The best human preparation possible should then be made for the crusade. All must be begun, continued, and ended in the spirit of earnest prayer. The elected chairmen of these ten crusade committees, along with the General Crusade Chairman, form the Crusade Steering Committee. This committee is responsible for the overall guidance and planning of the entire crusade effort in cooperation with the Crusade Field Director. Pastors of all participating churches serve as exofficio members of the Steering Committee.

The Prayer Committee

The work of the Prayer Committee is to enlist every person possible in praying daily for the crusade. Fervent prayer is a necessity in all soul-winning efforts. There are various plans being used to enlist people in prayer for a crusade. These have been proven successful.

A prayer card is a useful tool. One end could contain the evangelist's picture, crusade information, and a reminder to pray five minutes a day for the campaign. The opposite end of the card, could have a Scripture quotation about prayer, and a place for the person to sign a pledge to pray five minutes a day. Perforate the card in the center. (This idea was Dr. Chester Swor's.) The person who signs it tears off the pledge and drops it in the offering plate at the church. The other portion is placed in a conspicuous place at home as a reminder to pray daily for the crusade. It is beneficial for the pastor to preach on prayer and to distribute the prayer reminders about a month before the campaign begins. The card serves as a prayer reminder and keeps the crusade before the family.

A prayer calendar is also effective. Have an artist draw a picture of an old-fashioned clock and divide the 24 hour period into 15 minute sections. Try to get at least two people to pray at the same time during each 15 minute period throughout the day and night. This can be done for one day or for a week preceding the crusade.

Cottage or home prayer meetings prior to a crusade are productive; especially if a radio broadcast can be conducted in connection with the cottage prayer meetings. The broadcast should be advertised and conducted at the exact hour for the beginning of the prayer meeting. The speaker should conduct a devotional on prayer, revival, or soul winning. He should encourage people to go to these prayer meetings and pray.

Witness Committee

This Committee should be divided into three subcommittees.

The Counselor Subcommittee.—Personal workers should be secured and trained to counsel with all who make decisions and lead the lost to Christ. Most evangelists have mimeographed instructions for teaching these counselors. Classes should be conducted under the leadership of a soul-winning pastor or layperson prior to the campaign. The plan of salvation should be taught and instructions should be given for use of various Scriptures.

If possible, personal workers should be secured to do soul-winning from house to house, prior to and during the campaign. The names of lost people should be assigned to them. They should be sent out to win the lost and to bring them to the crusade to make a public confession of their faith. It is helpful to have counselors placed throughout the audience to assist in winning the lost to Christ during the invitation at the conclusion of the message. Well-trained personal workers are also needed to counsel with each person who responds to the invitation in the counseling center or inquiry room. These counselors should be placed in reserved seats, one counselor for each ten pews (one to each 100 seats) in the auditorium.

It is wise to have the counselors designated by a ribbon or in some other manner. Sometimes people who are not authorized to do personal work will attempt to help. There is danger in this. The people doing personal work in an audience should be approved by his pastor or by a committee. It is recommended that those doing personal work in a crusade should go through the prescribed training course. Pastors and others who have had training might be excused from the classes, but no one else. It is important for the personal workers to know what the Bible says about the way of salvation. Their character and reputation should be above reproach; they should be a stepping stone to lost souls in finding Jesus.

The Census or Prospect Subcommittee.—It is necessary to secure a list of names and addresses of prospects if an effective job is to be done in a crusade. The Bible commands us to "Go out into the highways and hedges" (Luke 14:23, KJV) and urge people to come to the gospel feast. We need to know under what hedge a person is hiding.

The names and addresses of lost people and unchurched people are needed so they can be assigned to the personal workers to visit during the crusade. The evangelist and/or the pastor of a participating church should also write them a personal invitation to attend the meetings.

The territory to be covered by a crusade should be divided into sections and volunteers asked to go from house to house to secure the desired information. Most denominations furnish cards on which the desired religious information can be secured in a census. After the cards have been secured, they should be classified and divided according to the streets as well as according to religious status and denominational preference.

In a citywide meeting, it is effective to assign the prospects who express denominational preferences to the personal workers of that denomination. In this way the group with whom they are in sympathy has a chance to seek to win them to Christ as well as to their fellowship.

The Follow-Up Subcommittee.—The results of many crusades do not last as they should because nothing is done to conserve the results. A committee should be appointed to carry out a program of encouraging every convert in his new commitment. The following should be done:

(1)　See that every pastor receives the names and addresses of those who express a desire to unite with his church or who live in the vicinity where his church meets.

(2)　Urge the pastor to contact the converts by telephone and letter.

(3)　Write a personal letter to those making decisions in the crusade and urge them to follow through with their decisions. Send them helpful literature.

(4)　Check on those making decisions to help them continue to live for Christ. This should be done through personal phone calls and letters from pastors and older Christians.

(5)　Every convert should be assigned to a "spiritual buddy." This person should be one who will promise to keep up with the convert's spiritual progress for at least three months. This suggestion works as follows: If a convert desires to join a given church, the pastor visits him and urges him to follow through by uniting with the church. Then the pastor chooses one of his most spiritual members, who is about the same age and is the same sex as the convert, and asks him if he will be a "spiritual buddy." A "spiritual buddy" makes friends with the new convert, visits him, and encourages him to read the Bible, to pray, and to attend Sunday school and church regularly. A report should be given to the pastor on the progress the new convert is making.

There are wonderful programs of discipleship and follow up available and used in many churches today. Some churches will have laypersons already trained and experienced not only in leading a person to Christ but also in building up that new Christian in the basic disciplines of the Christian life. At the training sessions where counselors are trained for the crusade, they should be taught how to have a quiet time with God, how to pray, how to study the Bible for personal instruction and growth, as well as how to share their faith. They need also to be taught how to teach new believers to do this.

Churches should be encouraged to train these "spiritual buddies" before the crusade. Then in every congregation men and women of spiritual depth will not only know how to share their faith but also how to teach newborn Christians the basic rudiments of Christian living.

If the new convert should begin to slip in his spiritual life, an immediate report should be given to the appropriate pastor. It is literally impossible for a pastor to receive scores of additions to his church in a crusade and then look out over his audience in the

Sundays to follow and check on all who are absent. One by one they can slip away without his knowing it. The "spiritual buddy" plan will prevent this.

The Publicity Committee

It is possible to have crusades without publicity, but in this day it is rare. The people need to know pertinent information about the campaign before they can be expected to attend. Today the radio, TV, movies, and many other attractions compete for the attention of the people. They must be sold on what is offered in the crusade.

Great care should be given in selecting the Publicity Committee. The general chairman should be a person with some knowledge of promotional and publicity work. If that is not possible, then the one entrusted with this work should seek the aid of experts. The average newspaper should have someone on staff who can help. Larger cities have advertising agencies. There are several companies specializing in advertising for churches and crusades. They can provide cheaper assistance than regular advertising agencies because they have already designed materials which can be adapted to the average crusade.

The publicity committee should consult the evangelist for his suggestions. Most evangelists have had experts prepare materials which can be furnished to the local committees. Since the costs of art, engraving, and other preparation of the original layouts are divided among several crusades, it is usually more economical to use advertising prepared for your evangelist.

• Newspaper publicity.—Newspapers are probably the best media for advertising. Good news stories and advertisements will pay big dividends in interest and attendance. As a rule, newspapers are cooperative. However, oftentimes they do not seem to be interested because they feel that the crusade offers no real news or because they fear the news stories will not be presented to them in a usable form.

Visiting the newspaper editor will provide an opportunity to ask him how to cooperate with him in using his columns for the crusade. Having pictures that are really news and new stories about the plans and progress of the crusade, will ensure that the paper will probably carry the items. They do not want to carry the items that are not really news. Discuss with the editor what is considered news. Have someone prepare the copy in the proper form and submit it to them ahead of their deadline for such copy.

Also, use the columns of the newspaper for well-prepared advertisements. Advertisement space is the principal source of revenue for the newspaper. Reciprocate their cooperativeness by purchasing advertisement space. Money spent in newspaper advertising is far from wasted. If the advertisements are properly prepared and placed in the paper at the proper time, they will produce good results. The average newspaper has an advertising manager who can help in the preparation of the copy. Try to place an advertisement in the paper a couple of weeks before the revival crusade begins, a week before it begins, and then the largest advertisement on the day the campaign actually starts. Advertisements can be placed in the paper daily during the crusade, and sometimes less frequently.

• Media.—Properly prepared spot announcements are effective on both radio and television. Check with the stations to find out rates and the time best suited for spot announcements.

It is wise to check all of the religious programs on the stations in the area and ask them to make announcements about the crusade. Check with a radio station about local news broadcasts. Every station has such programs at stated times throughout the day. They will carry your crusade free.

It is effective to have a daily radio broadcast prior to, and during, the crusade. Usually the ministers will give up the daily devotional period on the radio to the crusade, if they are asked to do so. The evangelist should be glad to conduct these programs during the campaign. Sometimes it is wise to buy a period prior to or following the daily devotional to give him thirty minutes for conducting a great evangelistic broadcast.

Television is usually expensive. However, if the talent can produce a top-notch program, then television is an effective medium to use for promoting the crusade. Cable television is an excellent option to live television.

• Bumper signs.—Pressure-sensitive bumper signs are popular and effective if properly used. Manufacturers are now making pressure-sensitive paper with messages printed on it. A local printer can provide information about the latest materials available and prepare bumper signs upon request.

• Brochures and Handbills.—Handbills are not as effective in this modern age, but if they are used, be sure they are properly designed and printed. If the crusade budget will allow, have an advertising firm prepare an attractive two-color brochure. Attractive folders can be secured that require only the local copy to be printed. Some denominational headquarters furnish such a service to their churches.

An attractive folder should be distributed to every house throughout the area to be reached by the crusade. These can be distributed in daily or weekly papers for a reasonable sum. The territory can be divided into sections and covered by youth distributing the folders from house to house.

It is generally a little more expensive, but it is effective to mail the folders to the homes of all local and rural postal patrons. This is done in conjunction with a letter written by the evangelist.

• Posters and Billboards.—Two-color posters with dimensions of either 11″ × 14″ or 14″ × 22″ are effective. Several companies specialize in this type of advertising.

• Street Banners.—Street banners are expensive but effective. Many evangelists have them prepared so that they will have to change only the date and place. Contact a sign painter about them. Usually permission must be secured to place them across city streets.

• Lapel Buttons or Ribbons.—These should be worn by those interested in the crusade. The wording must be proper and brief, and designed to encourage people to ask questions. There are firms that specialize in this type of publicity.

• Door Knob Hangers—Doorknob hangers can be printed by a good printer. They must be die cut to make them attractive and functional. An effective line to introduce your copy on these door knob hangers is: "Just Hanging Around to Invite You to Attend..." then give data about the crusade.

• Telephone Callers.—Either the week prior to the crusade or once the crusade is under way, a telephone campaign should be launched. A telephone directory can be cut into sections containing ten telephone numbers and pasted on cards to be distributed for people to call extending an invitation to the crusade. It is advisable to prepare a copy and suggest what they are to say. Sometimes it is wise to arrange to have every telephone user called twice during the crusade; perhaps once each week by a different person.

• Personal Letters.—A personal letter should be written to each family in the area where the crusade is to be conducted. Their names can be secured through census, or from the churches cooperating in the meeting. In some places, power companies and others possessing the names and addresses of the people living in the area will allow the use of their mailing list.

Many pastors write letters to their members encouraging them to support the crusade. In addition to this letter, there should be a letter from the evangelist. An appeal should be made to the Sunday School officers and teachers for additional support. Always include one of the brochures advertising the crusade along with other suitable material.

• Sound or Public Address System.—Some cities prohibit the use of a sound system on their streets. See if permission can be secured before engaging a public address system. If permission is given, this is an effective way to advertise a crusade prior to and during its progress.

The Special Groups Committee

General Duties.—This committee is to promote attendance of special groups from towns or cities both within and outside the immediate area of the crusade. They should contact local service clubs, labor groups, factories, and business firms to encourage them to attend. Often people, who otherwise might not attend, will attend to be loyal to their group or community. It is helpful to provide reserved sections for these groups.

Children's Service.—This committee should see special services are conducted for the children during the crusade. A children's service can be held from 15 to 30 minutes prior to the beginning of the main service. This can be under the direction of the evangelist, music director, children's worker of the team, or someone selected by the crusade team or the local committee.

A Children's Rally on Saturday mornings or afternoons during the crusade is effective. Some evangelists have found it best to conduct children's meetings every afternoon just after the close of school. The children should not be ignored. If they are interested, then their parents will be interested also. If the children stay home, their mothers and fathers will usually stay with them, and none of them are reached.

Other Groups.—Youth, senior adults, singles, etc., need to be targets for special emphasis.

The Music Committee

The music director of one of the cooperating churches or an outstanding choir member is usually the chairman of this committee. The duty of the committee is to enlist choir members from the various churches to sing during the campaign. This committee should arrange to have the choir ready to be trained by the special music director for the revival crusade.

This committee should secure the proper musical instruments and have them ready when the campaign begins. The music committee should also have all available local talent ready to be presented to the music director. They should not, however, have the special music planned. Most music directors in city-wide crusades desire to present their own musical programs.

The People-Serving Committee

This committee should be divided into two subcommittees.

Usher's Subcommittee.—This committee is responsible for enlisting, training, and scheduling ushers and parking attendants. It is the duty of the users to see that the people are properly welcomed and seated. In a crusade with thousands in attendance, this is quite a responsibility. The work requires special planning and execution if the crusade is to operate smoothly. Have at least one usher for every 50 seats in the crusade and place a reserved sign on a seat for each usher. This committee also has the responsibility of receiving the offering.

Parking attendants should be enlisted and trained to take care of the cars as they enter and leave the parking area. In our mobile society, with expensive cars and concern about safety, this is a most significant responsibility. Many people will not stay for a crusade or return if they are not properly parked, welcomed, and assisted as they try to leave.

Child Care Subcommittee.—It is imperative that child care be provided for small babies, and, if possible, for children up to three years of age. Parents with small children usually do not attend a crusade if a nursery is not provided.

The Child Care Subcommittee should secure a clean, comfortable place for the nursery, borrow necessary equipment, arrange for nurses, and so forth. One or two trained nurses can supervise the nursery. Seek out volunteers from the various churches to assist them.

The Attendance-Transportation Committee

This committee should be divided into two subcommittees that should correlate their work.

Transportation Subcommittee.—Many people do not have a way to get to a crusade. Car pools and church vehicles should be arranged to transport those desiring to attend. Secure vehicles from various sections of the community with space for one or more riders. Set up and advertise a telephone where people can call for a free ride. By proper organizations dozens and even hundreds of people, who otherwise might not attend, can be brought to the crusade every night. Hundreds of cars come to citywide crusades with empty seats. The possibilities for opportunities are unlimited for the transportation committee.

Attendance Subcommittee.—A successful method for encouraging attendance is to have "special nights" in a crusade, such as Sunday School Night, Family Night, Church Loyalty Night. It is the duty of the Special Nights Subcommittee to promote these night in the sponsoring churches.

The subcommittee should confer with the evangelist before scheduling the special nights. The evangelistic message should coordinate with the nightly emphasis. Here are some suggestions for nightly emphasis.

1. Sunday School at Night

Sunday School teachers are a great source for crusade promotion. They can be asked to get their own classes to attend every crusade service. They enlist the pupils, keep a record of their attendance at the crusade, contact them if absent, and seek to win them to Christ. Designated seats can be provided for each teacher and his or her class.

Write to the Sunday School teachers and officers weeks in advance of the beginning of the crusade and seek to enlist them in the plan. A detailed explanation of the plan is sent along with the record forms they are to keep on their classes. This plan divides the responsibility for promoting the crusade. Imagine what can happen when scores of teachers are working daily in the interest of the souls of their pupils.

2. Sunday School Rally Day

If the campaign is conducted in a single church, this rally should be conducted during the Sunday School on that day. All of the classes, from about nine years old and up, should meet in the auditorium and the evangelist should give them a brief but intense evangelistic message.

If the campaign is conducted on a citywide basis, then this rally should be conducted one week night each week of the crusade. The Sunday Schools of the sponsoring churches can sit behind their banners and be recognized by standing, or by a "head count." The service should be centered around trying to win the Sunday School members to Christ.

3. Other Promotional Ideas

Following are a number of promotional ideas used most

advantageously in a local church crusade that might be adapted to promote attendance at a citywide or area crusade.

• *"Don't Be a Black Sheep"*

In church crusades, the "Black Sheep" plan designed by the Tabernacle Press of Texas is very successful. Small cardboard sheep, black on one side and white on the other, are used to promote attendance at the big Sunday School rally. Each class is assigned a goal and given sheep to be signed. Members are asked to be a "white sheep" by signing their names and placing it in the "pasture" on the board. A large cardboard is drawn into sections or "pastures" for each class in a department. If a class has a goal of 25, that is how many sheep are in their "pasture." If 15 have signed up to attend, there will be 15 white sheep and 10 black sheep. As members sign up to attend the rally, the black sheep are turned over and the names of those agreeing to attend are placed on the white side. The cardboard with the sheep are placed where all can see them.

The appeal during the promotion is "Don't Be a Black Sheep." You can order the sheep or have them printed and die cut by a local printer.

• *"I Will Not Break the Chain"*

One of the most effective plans for obtaining a high attendance for Sunday School rally day or night is the chain link system. A link about one inch wide by eight and one half inches long can be mimeographed or printed. It reads:

I Will Not Break The Chain

Unless Providentially Hindered, I Will Be One Of
A Goal of 500 Attending The Sunday School Rally
At _____

On _____ a.m.

Signed_____

A small paper stapler can be used to make a chain of the links. By hanging this in a conspicuous place, the progress of the effort can be seen.

• *"I Will Be One Of The Bunch"*

Paper bananas are purchased or made with this wording imprinted: "I will be one of the bunch" attending the Sunday School rally. A stem is made up for those who sign to attend and the bananas are pinned on it. The appeal is "Get on a banana and slide in" with the bunch.

• *Fishing for Men Plan*

Buy, or make, cardboard fish with a place for those who are "caught" (agree to attend the service) to sign their names. Suggested wording for the themes "I'm On The Hook To Attend The Crusade Monday Night." String the fish and keep them before the people as you urge those helping to "Go Out, Fish for Men," or to "Get on the Hook" and attend.

• *My Friend and I Banquet*

The church sponsoring the crusade is to prepare a real banquet. Distribute free tickets. Any member can have as many tickets for free dinners for his friends as desired. The only requirement is, those brought must be either lost people, or church members who are prospects for local church membership. (Of course, the person bringing a friend does not tell him of this requirement. The banquet should be timed to end just as the crusade service begins. The members and their guests can conveniently attend the service.)

If the "Friend and I Banquet" is planned during a citywide crusade, then each church will conduct its own banquet and get its prospects to attend the meeting with the members inviting them.

• *Cradle Roll Night*

This plan works best in a single church crusade. Have someone take pictures of the babies of the area, especially those enrolled in the Cradle Roll department of the church. Show these pictures on "Cradle Roll Night." Tell the mothers and fathers that they are to be honored guests and the picture of their baby will be shown on the screen. Have them stand when their baby is recognized.

If a picture cannot be made, a nursery worker can walk across the front of the auditorium, carrying the baby as its name is called. Proud parents will enjoy a service with this recognition.

• *Pack the Pew Night*

Enlist volunteers to take pews on designated nights and seek to fill them with their friends. The "packers" could volunteer for each night, or set aside only one or two nights a week for this method. Give an award to the person bringing the most new people to pack the pews. Various organizations such as the Woman's Missionary Union or the Men's Brotherhood could also agree to pack the pews on different nights.

• *Family Night*

Seek to get every member of every possible family to attend.

Give special mention, or perhaps an award, to the family having the most members present. (Include distant relatives of the families to increase the number present.)

• *Men's Night, Women's Night, and Youth Night*

Emphasis on various groups provides special affirmation. One night can be Men's Night and have the men sing in the choir; another, Women's Night, when the women will be featured and "played against" the results of the Men's Night. Always have a Youth Night each week with a program designed to reach youth.

The Special Nights Committee should work on these and seek to get everyone enthusiastic about his special night. The purpose, of course, is not to play one group against another, but to get all groups to cooperate.

• *Church Organization Night*

The attendance on given nights can be sponsored by various church organizations. One night can be designated Sunday School Night, another Discipleship Training Night, Christian Endeavor or Youth Fellowship Night, and another Woman's Missionary Union Night. The chairman should recognize members of the various organizations on their special night.

• *Church Loyalty Night*

In citywide crusades, a Church Loyalty Night provides good results. Each church should sit together with their own banner. Urge each church to let their light shine on that night. Count the attendance from the various churches, or at least have them stand. Give an award to the church with the largest attendance or the largest percentage of their membership present.

• *Wiping the Slate Clean for Revival*

It is difficult to put aside other engagements in the interest of a revival. Rev. E. C. Abernathy, Jr., Of Tampa, Florida, sought to solve this problem in his church using this approach. Some weeks prior to the beginning of the crusade, have a large blackboard brought into the church auditorium. Across the top write the words: "WIPING THE SLATE CLEAN FOR REVIVAL." Underneath list several possible conflicts such as: "Club meetings," "Social Engagements," "Television Programs." Members of the church, can step to the blackboard and erase the word describing the conflict appropriate for them. As the conflicting engagements are erased, the person says: "I am wiping my slate clean of the obligations that conflict with the crusade." This allows for careful scheduling before the crusade begins.

Arrangements Committee

This committee should function in two subcommittees.

Facilities Subcommittee.—The duties of this subcommittee are to secure the location and tent or auditorium for the meetings. Details of seating, lighting, sound equipment should also be spelled out, as well as parking, rest room, and nursery facilities.

In a citywide crusade the work of this subcommittee is heavy. In areas where a city auditorium is not available, or where the auditorium cannot be secured, the subcommittee must secure a tent or make other provisions for seating the people. Usually tents can be rented from tent manufacturing companies. These companies also rent seat ends and other tent equipment. The housing committee should make contacts as quickly as possible after the date is set so as to be able to secure the needed equipment at the desired time.

Entertainment Subcommittee.—This subcommittee will secure a place for the crusade team to stay. They should inspect the motel or hotel before engaging any room. Whenever possible, private rooms should be provided, especially for the evangelists, song leader, and other members of the team who engage in full-time crusade work.

The evangelist should be consulted about entertainment. Most preachers do not care to eat a meal in the evening prior to the service. It is unfair and unwise to overestimate the speaker's needs for entertainment. The crusade party is in the community, not to be entertained, but to work for God. Every detail should be planned with the thought of enabling them to do their best for God in the crusade.

Community Involvement Committee

It is advantageous to couple the actual crusade services with other planned outreach opportunities. Special guest appearances at the crusade should also be arranged and scheduled. The evangelist, singer, and special guests could make appearances at civic clubs, schools, industries, on radio, television, and other sources of community outreach.

Finance Committee

A well-selected committee should be in charge of the finances of a crusade. This committee should work out a budget for the crusade with the pastors and evangelist. All funds collected should be counted by members of the committee (never by a single member alone) and banked.

Select a member of the Finance Committee as treasurer for the crusade. The general chairman and local pastor should be informed from night to night about the amount of the offerings taken, the amount of the budget, and the amount of money needed to cover expenses.

The Finance Committee should design a fast, dignified way of taking the offerings in the services. Plans should be made in conference with the chairman of the ushers and the general chairman. A popular method is to use half-gallon ice cream containers because they are cheap. One is provided for each row of 50 seats in the auditorium. A stack of ten containers is placed at each usher's seat. When the offering is taken the usher walks from row to row and gives a container to the first person at the end of each row, with a motion to pass it down the row. An usher at the other end of the row collects the containers. The entire audience can be covered in about two minutes.

Every person involved with the finances—including the crusade party—should strive to keep expenses as low as possible without hurting the efficiency of the program. Information concerning finances should be available to everyone responsible for the crusade. Responsible handling of money is an absolute necessity. The Finance Committee should have its books audited at the close of the campaign and send a mimeographed report to all cooperating churches. By keeping the churches informed, their confidence and cooperation is retained for future crusades.